Rien ne va plus

Rien Ne Va Plus

by

MARTIN CRAWSHAY

The Memoir Club

© Martin Crawshay 2002

First published in 2002 by
The Memoir Club
Whitworth Hall
Spennymoor
County Durham

All rights reserved.
Unauthorised duplication
contravenes existing laws.

British Library Cataloguing in
Publication Data.
A catalogue record for this book
is available from the
British Library.

ISBN: 1 84104 044 4

Typeset by George Wishart & Associates, Whitley Bay.
Printed by Bookcraft (Bath) Ltd.

*To Grania, without whose patience,
encouragement and good sense
I would not have survived.*

Contents

List of Illustrations ix
Foreword xi
Preface xiii

Chapter 1	Early Days	1
Chapter 2	Aldeburgh Lodge and Orwell Park	9
Chapter 3	Eton	16
Chapter 4	I Join the Army	28
Chapter 5	My Commissioned Service	36
Chapter 6	Betwixt and Between	47
Chapter 7	The Horserace Betting Levy Board – Inception	52
Chapter 8	The Horserace Betting Levy Board – Dismissal	58
Chapter 9	The Horserace Betting Levy Board – The Wigg Years	66
Chapter 10	The Horserace Betting Levy Board – Discrimination Continues	85
Chapter 11	The Horserace Betting Levy Board – Sir Desmond Plummer	101
Chapter 12	The Horserace Betting Levy Board – A Different Atmosphere	110

Chapter 13	The Suffolk Red Cross and Other Charitable Work	123
Chapter 14	Reflections	131
Appendix I	Case History, 12 July 1972	138
Appendix II	Retirement Speech, 25 July 1991	150
Appendix III	Letters in Facsimile	157
Index		167

List of Illustrations

At Eton, 1941 18
Escorting Her Majesty the Queen during the
    inspection of the Oxford University Air Squadron,
    4 November 1960 44
Wedding Day, 24 October 1967 68
The Horserace Betting Levy Board Staff, 1983 111
The Horserace Betting Levy Board, 1987 112
Presenting a Levy Board premium to Mr Jim Salt,
    owner of the Supreme Champion at the National
    Shire Horse Stallion Show, 1983 117
Presenting a trophy to Miss Sydney Smith at the
    National Hackney Breed Show, 1989 118
At the Levy Board office, 1991 120
At Home, 1997 124
With Christopher Whybrow and Toby at a Red Cross
    garden, 2000 126
The author at the awards ceremony arranged by the
    National Blood Service at the University Arms Hotel,
    Cambridge, 23 August 2001 128
In South Africa, 1992 132
Richard's Aunt Betty, the author, Richard Gisborough
    and Toby Chalonor in South Africa, 1992 132
Playing croquet with Charlie, 1992 135
With Lennox Hannay at Spring Hill, 1993 136

Foreword
by Julian Wilson

WITHOUT DOUBT, the early days of the Horserace Betting Levy Board were amongst the most important and significant periods in recent turf history.

When the Betting and Gaming Act of 1960 legalized off-course cash betting, LBOs (licensed betting offices) sprang up like mushrooms. Although, as the author reveals, bookmakers claimed that the majority of bets were for no more than sixpenny (2½p) stakes and that the business was cost-intensive, the flamboyant Glaswegian, John Banks, was more forthcoming in describing betting shops as a 'licence to print money'. Accordingly, the major bookmaking firms soon became multi-million pound public companies, with the brand leaders Ladbrokes buying the Hilton Group and becoming international hoteliers.

Meanwhile, the Horserace Betting Levy Board had been established by statute principally to compensate the racing industry for lost revenues at racecourses, and through the Tote. The reasons why racing has never received an equitable return from betting, as bookmakers year after year outmanoeuvred the Levy collectors, are revealed lucidly in the author's fascinating account of the Board's early years. In the post-war era, racing administration was viewed as a resettlement area for ex-army officers who became starters, judges, handicappers and Clerks of the Course. Unhappily, the same qualifications were regarded as suitable for membership of the Levy Board with, in some cases, disastrous results.

This book is a delight to read, encompassing pre-war countryside life; Eton during the war years; the hardship of rationing; the austere regime of the post-war army; and the restrictive exclusiveness of going racing in the forties, fifties and early sixties, when a voucher signed by a Jockey Club member was a prerequisite to admission to the Members' Enclosure at Newmarket Races.

Whilst the author and I shared many friends, notably the late Lord Kilmany and my Suffolk neighbour Douglas Kaye, we also shared an implacable enemy in Lord Wigg. The story of Wigg's chairmanship of the Board – a classic case of the curate's egg – recalls the most public conflict in racing's post-war history. The enmity between Wigg and the Duke of Norfolk came to a head when Norfolk spoke over the loud speakers at Ascot (paid for by the Levy Board!) condemning his rival and the way that Levy money was spent. Wigg responded by likening the Earl Marshal, and the Jockey Club in general, to 'a well-kept vintage motor car'.

In his twenty-eight years at the Board the author was to shoulder the burden of several unsuitable Chairmen, including the ex-Railways and Gaming Board chief Sir Stanley Raymond, who referred in his introductory Press Conference to 'the great Leslie Piggott' [*sic*]. A shrewd backer of horses in his younger days, the author maintains the old-fashioned virtues of good manners and decency and tells the story of an era that saw everyday standards slip gradually into terminal decline.

Preface

I WAS SURPRISED on my 73rd birthday to receive a letter from the Memoir Club suggesting that I should write the story of my life. The letter said that in their opinion I had had an interesting life and assured me of all the support I would need with the project. I did not reply immediately but the letter reminded me that, at the time of my retirement from the Horserace Betting Levy Board, a number of people had suggested that I write a history of that organization. I knew that this would not be possible, first because the authorities would not allow me access to all the papers which I would need, and second because if I were to write in detail about the various conflicts which had been a feature of a divided industry, I would lose a number of friends late in life. Friends are important and, while I had been a party to so many endless negotiations, I never had the inclination to go over it all again and point a finger at people who had done their best even if they had failed.

The suggestion from the Memoir Club was, however, different. The suggestion was that I should write the story of my entire life which, they claimed, would be of a wide enough interest to give adequate satisfaction. I had been brought up in a house lit mainly by oil lamps; I had been brought up to believe in the British Empire; I had experienced the Second World War; conditions at school and in the army had changed out of all recognition; I had worked for twenty-eight years in the Horserace Betting Levy Board where certain aspects of administration would scarcely be believed; yes, there was indeed a story, and the proposal had arrived just as I had finished nine years' service with the Suffolk Red Cross. I once again needed something to do.

I decided to fall in with the Memoir Club who, in a second letter, told me that my service with the Levy Board was a principal reason for their making the approach. I told the Memoir Club that my story would be my own personal experiences and would in no way be a history of the Board.

I was fortunate in that I had retained copies of the Board's Annual Reports throughout my service and, because of the scandalous discrimination which had prevailed, I had kept two identical personal files recording the events which affected me. The reason for having two files was that I needed to be safeguarded in case one was stolen or lost.

Horseracing politics are as nasty as any other form of politics and the divisions within the racing industry still continue with the same intensity as they have done for many years, leading me to believe that the horse, which should bring us closer together, divides us in a way that other animals do not. My appreciation of the Levy Board stems from the fact that in twenty-eight years I never had a dull day, and it provided me with the greatest challenge of my life. Everyone is tested at some time or other, and you do not know yourself until you are faced with extreme circumstances. My extreme circumstances came in the wake of George Wigg and his appointees.

This story is therefore written mainly for the interest of my descendants, to describe a world which has changed for ever, and also to express my appreciation to a number of people, both within and outside the Levy Board, who helped me to overcome and recover from the traumatic experiences between 1966 and 1975.

Martin Crawshay
Leavenheath

CHAPTER 1

Early Days
1928-1937

THE CRAWSHAYS, originally from Normanton in Yorkshire, were pioneers of the Industrial Revolution and were, for four generations, the leading ironmasters of their time. Their business was developed from 1780 by my great-great-great-great-grandfather, Richard Crawshay, who, after a disagreement with his father, had left Yorkshire aged 16 to make his fortune. This he did by negotiating his way into the iron trade in South Wales. At the end of the eighteenth century he employed 1,500 men and his Cyfartha works, the biggest in the world, were visited by Lord Nelson and Lady Hamilton. Money was made principally by the sale of munitions in the Napoleonic wars and, later, by the sale of railway track all over the world in the great railway boom. A grant of arms was awarded on 2 March 1793 when Richard visited the College of Arms with a portrait of his guard dog at the Cyfartha works. This portrait is in my possession.

By the time of his death in 1810 he had become sole owner of the Cyfartha Ironworks in Merthyr Tydfil and was, according to the *Sunday Times*, the twelfth richest man in this country. The Crawshays were never, and never pretended to be, aristocrats, other than aristocrats of industry. They put principle before money and lived close to their workers, most of whom they knew by name. Richard's son, William (1764-1834), also sole owner of Cyfartha, had three sons, the eldest of whom, also called Richard, was my great-great-grandfather.

This Richard (1786-1859), while retaining an interest in the selling of iron through the London House in Upper Thames Street, had no responsibility for the works at Cyfartha, which fell to his younger brother William (1788-1867). He became a landowner, purchasing Ottershaw Park in Surrey in 1842 and leasing Honingham Hall in Norfolk, and founding a Crawshay's Brewery in Norwich. This led to my family's association with the Crown Brewery in King Street, Norwich, which was to last for five generations and resulted in 1897 with the formation of Youngs, Crawshay & Youngs, of which my great-grandfather, grandfather and father were all Chairman.

It is my grandfather's Georgian house at Witton off the Norwich-to-Yarmouth road near Brundall which provides my earliest memories. In the early 1930s my father was still serving in the army, although he had become a Director of our Norwich brewery, which at that time was still possible for a serving officer. The family all tended to congregate at Witton, where my grandfather retained a staff which included four gardeners and two chauffeurs, Hector and Clifford. In those days all male employees were always referred to only by their surnames. We children enjoyed what seemed to us to be a large garden and spent as much time with the servants as we did with our parents. It was here that I got to know Thomas Adderson, who had been with my grandfather since the First World War and had worked his way up from stable-hand to footman, and then butler. He had married Florrie, the cook, but sadly they had no children. After my grandfather's death, they worked for my aunt (his daughter) and so their whole lives were devoted to the Crawshay family. In those days a footman would be in the dining room during meals and listened to the conversation of his employer and guests. It was because of this that I learned from Adderson a story of my great-great-grandfather, Richard Crawshay of Ottershaw Park, which he had learned from my grandfather who was a raconteur and had a fund of stories.

When Richard Crawshay died at Ottershaw in 1859, his butler sent a telegram (the service was then in its infancy) to his son Charles, my great-grandfather, who lived at Hingham near Norwich. The telegram, which was brought out from Norwich by horse, read, 'Come at once; your father has tumbled down dead in the park'. Charles installed the clock in Hingham Church in 1887 in recognition of the Golden Jubilee of Queen Victoria, and there are plaques in memory of him and his family in the north-east of the church.

Other memories of Witton were a lovely croquet lawn, sumptuous black grapes and electricity, which was not to be available in my father's house until he moved in 1945.

My grandfather, whose wife had died in 1928, the year in which I was born, always credited my child's bank account at Harrods with £5 on each birthday and at Christmas, and this would be equivalent to about £200 today. He was never happier than when in Norfolk and with his friends out shooting, or at Bungay or Yarmouth races. Two cars went to the races, and hence the need for two chauffeurs. The first car carried the family and guests and the second car was for any servants and the lunch. When he died in 1934, special writing paper and envelopes edged in black were ordered in accordance with the custom which prevailed at that time.

Witton House was left to my father who declined it, and so it was sold, with the proceeds going to my brother, Julian. Soon afterwards it was burned to the ground and was never rebuilt.

My father had by then retired from the army and leased a house at Croxton north of Thetford for £60 a year from the Crown Estates. This was convenient for his passion for shooting, for going to Newmarket and for attending to his duties at the brewery, to which he went on Wednesdays and Saturdays, having succeeded his father as Chairman. Croxton Lodge was a modest flint house at the north end of the village which had no electricity, but it did have its own gasometer. In order to make it adequate for his purposes my father installed a second bathroom and a downstairs lavatory. We were one of about half a dozen residents out of a population of some 250 who had a telephone, and into this comparatively small house were crammed my mother and father, my brother and I and my nanny, a living-in cook and two living-in housemaids who each had a room in the attics. Since there was no electricity most of the lighting was by way of paraffin lamps and only the principal rooms were lit by gas, which was made by my father from carbide. Although he employed a gardener who might have been expected to do this, my father preferred to do it himself and often the lights would flicker in the evening and he would have to stop whatever he was doing and go out to the gasometer and make some more.

My mother would visit the kitchen once a day to discuss the meals with the cook, and the details were written down on a slate. My parents changed for dinner every evening, my father wearing his smoking jacket and my mother wearing an evening dress. The housemaids were extremely smart, with an apron and white cap as was the custom for that period. Everything was done for us and even the drawing-room curtains were drawn at dusk by one of the housemaids. This was the ritual which had prevailed for generations in houses where servants were employed and this continued in most such houses until the outbreak of the Second World War. There were no weekly visits by the dustman in rural areas and most houses had their own refuse area and disposed of their own rubbish. There was very little packaging, which reduced the amount to be disposed of, and tradesmen delivered on certain days each week, which meant that many households, nearly all of whom grew their own vegetables, managed without visits to the shops. In Croxton there was a bus one day a week to Thetford and this enabled those who needed supplies to go to the town and find whatever was wanted. Since there was no electricity there were no refrigerators, and houses used to have a larder on the north side with a stone slab which remained cool and in which perishable food was stored. My father was not satisfied with this and obtained a small refrigerator which operated in the cellar using a paraffin lamp. It was very small and was really useless since it took two days to make a small amount of ice.

Drinking water was pumped by hand from one of the two deep wells located in the garden, and hot water was supplied from a coke boiler which never went out. Coal fires burned in every room, including the bedrooms, and I always enjoyed the flickering of the flames after my nursery light had been put out. A 'copper' in the scullery provided for some basic boiling, while sheets and smarter clothes were sent to the laundry in Bury St Edmunds. While it almost shames me to think of it today, my father took possession in 1935 of a very large Rolls-Royce which he retained for the remainder of his life and which was maintained in immaculate condition at the brewery. This car was, on occasions, made available for weddings in the village.

Dogs were part of the family and became my greatest friends. My mother did her best for the garden, which was home to masses of small birds and butterflies on a scale which is unbelievable today. We bicycled to swim in the Little Ouse at Six Mile Bottom, two miles downstream from Thetford, or in the lake at Fowl Mere adjacent to the Merton Hall Estate. I do not suppose anyone swims in either today, but to us it was all the greatest fun. We bicycled everywhere and I knew nearly all the families in the village and with other children we spent hours watching the trains between Thetford and Ely and placed pennies on the line. Nobody worried about us and we were totally safe, and I do not recall a single incident of anxiety or misbehaviour. Each holidays my brother and I would bicycle the 25 miles across country to Stowmarket to stay with my aunt for a few days and bicycle back again taking our few requirements with us. Our bicycles were equipped with gadgets such as speedometers and cyclometers to tell us how far we had gone.

As today, the farming in the area was principally arable and we spent long summer evenings helping while the corn was being cut. Both my brother and I were taught to shoot at an early age and I became quite an expert by the time I was 10 at shooting rabbits with a .410. The rabbits came bounding out as the size of each cornfield gradually diminished. We all cleaned our own catch, and up until the first outbreak of myxomatosis in 1953 rabbit was normal fare in most houses in the country, particularly during the Second World War. Most local people worked on the land or on the railway.

Attendance at church for Matins each Sunday at 11 a.m. was *'de rigueur'*, and the local farmer, who was the only other resident of the village to own a car, read the lessons with great vigour. Christmas Day was traditional and we did not receive our presents until after lunch; they were laid out on the piano and handed out one by one by my mother. My father had been brought up by his mother to always go to church every Sunday, and my grandmother kept a copy of Nelson's prayer in his cabin before the battle of Trafalgar in 1805. I have the prayer in my own prayer book now and it reads as follows:

> May the great God whom I worship grant to my country and for the benefit of Europe in general a great and glorious victory and may no misconduct in anyone tarnish it and may humanity after victory be the predominant feature in the British Fleet. For myself individually I commit my life to him who made me and may his blessing light upon my endeavours for serving my country faithfully. To him I resign myself and the just cause which is in trust to defend. Amen, Amen, Amen.

I think this prayer gives us much to think about in our materialistic world today.

At the age of seven I remember a rude shock when I was suddenly told I would be attending a kindergarten in Thetford. I am sure I enjoyed it, and once again the journey of two miles each way was usually undertaken by bicycle in the company of my nanny. The curriculum was probably no different from a similar establishment today, with emphasis on good behaviour and mixing with other children. I am told I once caused a stir at the school when, on being asked what I would like to drink I replied, 'Port or sherry, please'. This prompted the school's owner to bicycle out to see my mother who said that it reflected my father's indulgence of giving me a glass of port each Sunday.

CHAPTER 2

Aldeburgh Lodge and Orwell Park
1937-1941

I WAS SENT TO Aldeburgh Lodge for the summer term of 1937. I was 9 years old, which was slightly later than for most of my contemporaries. Both my father and my brother had been at Wixenford (now Ludgrove) but a change of headmaster, and perhaps because my mother wanted me nearer to home, meant that I was destined for the Suffolk School. Aldeburgh Lodge advertised itself as being a school for Norfolk and Suffolk boys and most came from these two counties although there were a few from elsewhere. I only spent two terms at Aldeburgh and my memories are restricted to walks on the North Fields, looking for amber and cornelians on the beach, and compulsory swimming in the North Sea. Nobody drowned and nobody complained, but what school would dare to march boys into the North Sea today? Aldeburgh Lodge no longer exists and its place has been taken, with a view over the sea, by a block of flats. The school's purpose was, of course, to prepare boys for the Common Entrance examination for all the major public schools. The school placed much emphasis on religious instruction, with close attention to the Authorized Version of the Bible, and anyone with a flair for cricket or indicating a career in the Royal Navy was sure to benefit from special attention.

In early 1938 the school moved to palatial Orwell Park

which, with its spacious grounds and playing fields, was a wonderful setting for educating young boys. The joint Headmasters, M.E. Wilkinson and J.F. Spurgeon, were delighted with the new environment. On the earliest possible occasion Mr Spurgeon gathered the school together in the Assembly Hall to welcome us to our new surroundings where he told us that he had been warned that he had been ill-advised to buy such a lovely house as the boys would be sure to damage it and mark the walls with ink. Of course we did no such thing and we took pride in where we were and realized how fortunate we were to be in such wonderful surroundings.

A feature of Orwell Park in 1938 was the Observatory which housed a telescope which in size was second only to Greenwich. Few other boys had the opportunity at such an early age to examine the planets and stars and to learn the rudiments of astronomy.

Orwell Park was an immensely happy school and in some ways was way ahead of its time. There were approximately 60 boys in this large country house where the dormitories were large and mostly overlooked the park and every boy had his own wash-basin.

One episode will remain with me forever. Although strictly forbidden, one of the excitements was to 'bounce' on one's bed after Matron had said goodnight. The higher the bounce, the greater the achievement. One unfortunate boy, David West, who was a particularly good bouncer, eventually not only smashed the springs of his bed in Arbutus dormitory, but sliced through most of his tongue as well. His pain and the sight of his tongue put an end to this activity for a long time.

The prospect, and the eventual declaration, of war with

Germany was followed in detail. Some of the staff had been involved in the Great War of 1914 to 1918 and the wounds from that awful conflict had not yet healed. Remembrance Day, which then was always on 11 November, was a sombre occasion and young minds were made aware of what it was all about. The Munich crisis of 1938 came and the Prime Minister, Mr Chamberlain, was considered a hero for returning with his piece of paper and peace in our time. When war came in 1939 we were taught to play our part. We grew vegetables, we drilled, we saved, and above all we believed in what our country was doing. The disasters of 1940 were followed in detail and I well remember Mr Spurgeon, who had great faith in the French army, assuring us that the line would be held, even as one French general was followed by another.

The possibility of invasion was of concern to all and the school moved in 1940, first to Hembury Fort near Honiton in Devon where we were joined by about five girls who had brothers in the school and where we swam in the River Otter, and then after one term to Bedstone Court in Shropshire where it remained for the remainder of the war. I think we must have moved from Orwell Park in a hurry, because a swimming-pool was being built but was not completed. Half-terms were cancelled and few parents were able to visit Bedstone Court as petrol supplies dwindled, but my own father did once bicycle the 28 miles from Shrewsbury, having come by train from Norwich. Letters became even more important. Envelopes were scarce and had to be used over and over again with the aid of an economy label. I competed with a boy called Michael Falcon, later to be a prominent businessman and High Sheriff of Norfolk, whose parents lived in Acle, to see whose envelope would survive the longest: his envelope crossed England twenty-eight times; such was the way we economized during the Second World War.

The outbreak of war had changed everything for ever. The servants had left and I well remember my father's actual words: 'Thank God they have gone.' He had his freedom in his own house at last. With Germany completing its conquest of most of Europe, prospects were decidedly gloomy but the thought of defeat was out of the question. The first two lines of the school song were particularly appropriate: 'Nil desperandum boys, stick to the rule; never give in for the sake of the School!' Those lines and my family motto of 'Perseverance' have helped me many times and I have realized that, in some form or other, life is one long battle.

Empire Day on 24 May was always a holiday and extra holidays were given whenever a boy won a scholarship to a major public school. Loyalty to the King, loyalty to the school and to each other was the basis of all our activities and most memories were of a happy existence with much appreciation for the way we were treated and encouraged. My achievements were modest. I was in the cricket eleven for my final term and I won something called the Fremantle Cup for sharpshooting on the rifle range in 1940, and I was sad to learn many years later that this cup was stolen along with other silver which, of course, could not be replaced. I also once won the competition for the best collection of butterflies and moths.

If the joint Headmasters had been asked at the time who would be the most successful boy of our generation they might well have selected Jim Prior, who was later to become a Cabinet Minister in Mrs Thatcher's Government and

Chairman of GEC. He was a good all-rounder and showed leadership qualities at an early age. He was a few months older than me, having been born in 1927, whereas I and most of my friends were born in 1928. When the time came for Common Entrance I passed into Lower Fourth at Eton, which was a disappointment to my father who had taken Upper Fourth and had won several prizes in his day at Wixenford as well as at Eton.

At Orwell Park I benefited in particular from excellent teaching in French and an understanding of the principal stories of the Bible. I realized later how much Mr Spurgeon had enjoyed analysing Genesis and anything with an element of blood and thunder. He also enjoyed instilling into young minds some useful phrases which most of us remembered all our lives. One was that until we had arrived at school we had only existed and now were going to live. Another was, 'Never knock anything down unless you put something better in its place', and a third was 'Even a fool can be thought a wise man if he keeps his mouth shut'. He would not have thought much of the bureaucracy which prevails today.

My parents' bitter divorce occurred while I was at Orwell Park. Children are adaptable and I had to adapt quickly to unusual circumstances. My mother left home of her own accord in 1938 and had to provide for herself. The divorce proceedings were long and unpleasant, and I did not enjoy being drawn into a quarrel in which I did not wish to adjudicate and in which I had no influence. From the moment of separation I did not have a normal home, and this mattered and affected me. Other members of the family seemed careful not to take sides, and I am of the view that my parents were incompatible. Once the separation had taken place, my parents never spoke to each other again and it was my job to divide the holidays in half and inform each parent when I would be arriving and leaving. My mother, despite her financial weakness, managed to arrange wonderful holidays. I was taught to ride in the New Forest and we were in Devon on 3 September 1939 at the outbreak of the Second World War. I can see us all now, sitting at a table and listening to the Prime Minister, Neville Chamberlain, saying that we were at war with Germany. My mother had lost her brother in 1918 (Brian Osborne, awarded the Military Cross, whose name is recorded on the Grenadier Guards Memorial at the foot of Lupton's Tower at Eton) and now, besides her own difficulties, she had to contemplate the future for her sons aged 16 and 11 as a further conflict developed. My mother displayed a photograph of Brian in uniform in her drawing-room for the rest of her life.

One particular incident arising from the divorce was rather poignant. It was a duty for children at boarding school to write a letter to their parents once a week. In my case I had to write two letters. On one occasion I must have written the usual two letters and placed them in the wrong envelopes. In my letter to my mother I had particularly asked if I could have riding lessons in the Christmas holidays; I was amazed when I got home to Croxton to find that my father, who had not ridden for many years, had arranged for two horses and a groom to be accommodated at the public house next door, so that we could go riding together every day. I realized what had happened and I was, of course, immensely touched that this should have been arranged for me.

My father remarried in 1942 and my half-sister, Virginia, was born in 1943. My father achieved domestic happiness, but the high taxation and difficulties relating to his business were to leave him an unhappy man for most of the rest of his life. My mother did not remarry and struggled alone, but did achieve happiness for her final years when living next to my brother in Norfolk and being proud of her four grandchildren. She died in 1972 aged 78. She had a great capacity for friendship, particularly for those who were in any way disadvantaged, and was particularly kind to Virginia who had lost both her parents by the time she was 16 and who spent much of her time as a teenager living at Tasburgh with Julian and Ann.

CHAPTER 3

Eton
1941-1946

I ARRIVED AT Eton for the Michaelmas Half (term) in September 1941 and was probably the smallest of the 250 or so new boys, and therefore the smallest boy in the School. I was 4ft 8in and weighed 5st 6lb. I was, of course, in 'jackets' since you were not supposed to be in 'tails' until you reached 5ft 4in, although for economic reasons some discretion was allowed.

I will never forget my first two days. I arrived with my father at the same house which my brother had left at the end of the previous half. I joined three other new boys for tea with the Dame (Matron). All of us no doubt were nervous and anxious to please, but my father, himself an Old Etonian, had made the unforgivable mistake of introducing me in shorts. If H.M. Bateman had been around he would have produced a drawing to double his well-deserved fortune. I never got round to asking my father why he had done this but I have always assumed it must have been some sort of economy. This error would have been soon forgotten but for one of the other new boys, Lennox Hannay, who was subsequently my best man, thinking it was so hilarious that the story had to be preserved and presented to all and sundry whenever the opportunity occurred. Being a good-natured fellow I never told him to drop it, and it continued to such an extent that my son's best man at his wedding in 2000 also had to tell a large audience all about it, to roars of laughter.

The second day was no better than the first. No one had taught me how the lovely white collar which accompanied jackets should appear over the coat and as worn by choristers. Fortunately, another small boy, soon to become a friend, saw my mistake and tucked his fingers underneath my collar and wrenched it into position and thus prevented further embarrassment. These are, of course, small things, but they are errors which should always be averted by those whose job it is to ease the path of adolescence. It was only on my second day that I realized how alone I was and how quickly I had to learn in order to survive in what was a strange environment. Orwell Park had not sent a boy to Eton during the previous five years and there were no relations or friends from home. Each new boy was given another slightly older boy to look after him and guide him in the labyrinth of jargon and geography which determined day-to-day activity. I was always a good mixer and, in spite of my size, I was determined not be overwhelmed by the magnitude of my new environment, but I much welcomed the guidance which was available. My father had given me little advice and no account of his own experiences between 1907 and 1912 other than to tell me that he had once been instructed by his fag master to sit on the lavatory seat until it was warm.

I was in what was reputed to be one of the best houses at that time. Our tutor, Hubert Hartley, who had rowed in the Cambridge Eight, was away for the war and returned only for my last half. His place was taken by Francis Cruso who had been a King's Scholar and who was steeped in the classics. He read beautifully and was undoubtedly a gifted

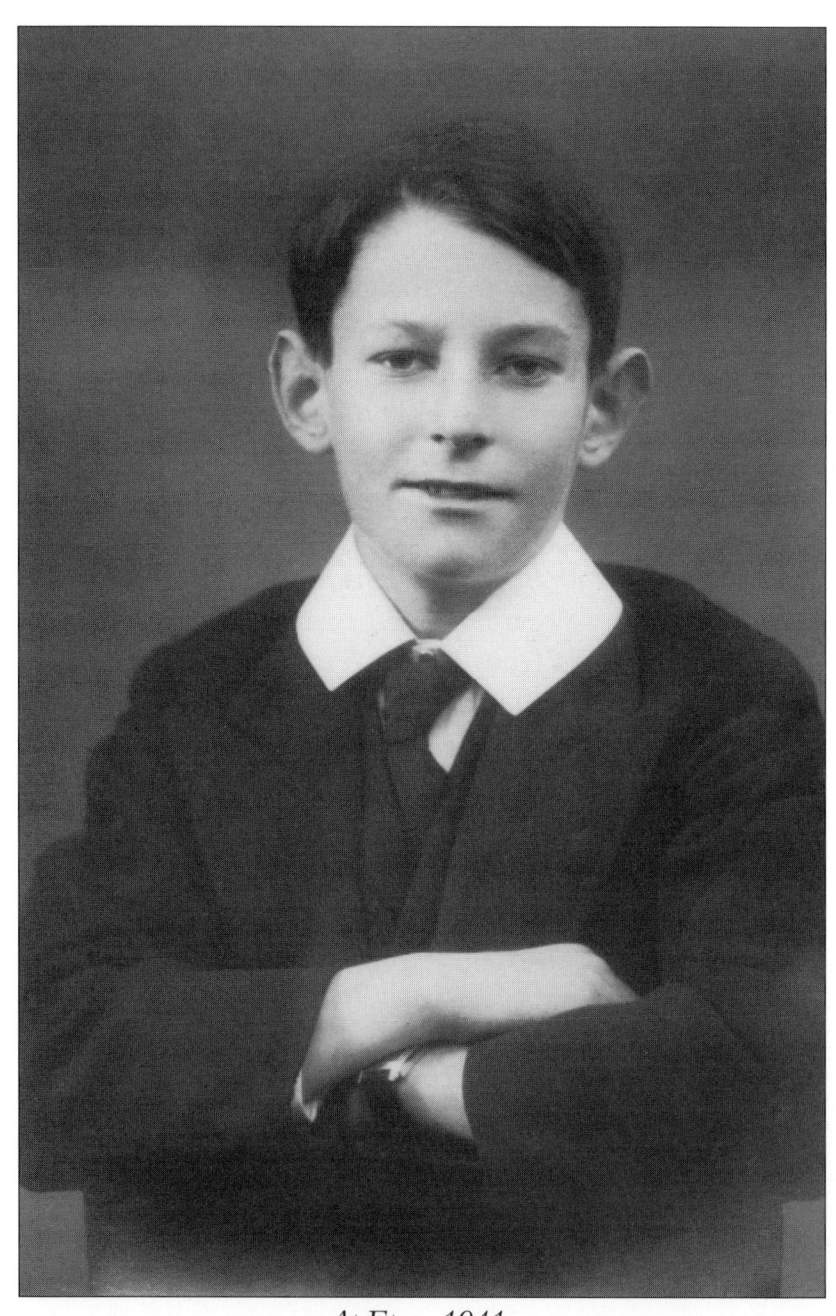

At Eton, 1941.

teacher. Grizel Hartley, wife of Hubert, was an Eton character known to all and to whom we were all 'darlings'. Hubert and Grizel had no children of their own and they devoted their attention and what money they had to the boys in their house. The result was much loyalty and friendships which have endured to this day. We were reputed to be the best-fed house in the school and our rations were supplemented by venison and other delicacies donated by friends. One unusual characteristic of the house was that the Library (prefects) had draught beer, drawn by the house butler, every day, and other senior boys had beer on Saturdays and Sundays.

Eton, like any other school, never was, and probably still is not, suitable for all boys. It has, however, excelled in giving those who go there confidence in themselves and qualities of leadership. This may have resulted in their being criticized for arrogance, but it is because neither the masters nor the boys were prepared to accept sub-standard work or suffer fools. There was always too much at stake, and Etonians were taught to strive for the best, and five years in elite surroundings with wonderful facilities are bound to leave their mark. Other schools have followed this example and the country is undoubtedly the better for it. Service to King (or Queen) and Country has always been at the top of the agenda and thirty-six Victoria Crosses, from the Battle of the Alma in 1854 to Goose Green in the Falklands in 1982, out of a total of 1,354 awarded to date, are evidence of outstanding bravery and sacrifice.

Because of my parents' divorce and because of war-time restrictions I had more fun at school than I did at home. There were friendships and many different activities, and the challenges which I faced were much to my liking. At the end of my first half I did well in trials (exams) and secured 'a double remove' which took me to Upper Fourth and thus one less half as a Lower Boy and one less half's fagging. This success was, however, somewhat dented by my mathematics master, a Mr Kerry, who in his report suggested I had 'most of the faults of the inky lower boy'. I later realized that he applied this description to many of his pupils and it had not been reserved specifically for me.

Fagging was very much the order of the day and it was no doubt good for boys from privileged homes to do menial tasks for others. In the winter months this involved lighting your fag master's fire and carrying a coal scuttle, which had been prepared by the odd-job man, to his room. Only one house out of twenty-four had central heating at that time and every boy had a fire in his own room. Lighting the fire was assisted by use of a 2ft sq 'blower' which, held against the chimney, ensured that the fire roared until it was well alight. It is extraordinary that in those old buildings with so many fires there was not a tragic accident.

Being so very small resulted in my once being fagged in the street. This was a privilege reserved only for a small number of very senior boys, and we knew who these were. The person concerned was Edward Boyle, then Captain of the Oppidans, who needed some message carried somewhere immediately, and seeing me he said, 'Are you by any chance a Lower Boy?' I could not deny it and hastened to do his bidding. He was an extremely nice boy, later to succeed to a baronetcy and to be a minister in Harold Macmillan's Government. I am sure that if I had said I was already doing something rather important, he would have found someone else.

There have been massive changes at Eton and other

schools since my day, and Eton has prided itself on being ahead of the game. Change, as in other aspects of life, came slowly. Inevitably, in a school which had survived every upheaval over some 500 years and which had so much history, there were any number of traditions. One was that you were not a proper Etonian until you had drunk from the school pump (in the Cloisters), had walked to the Copper Horse (statue of King George III in Windsor Great Park), and had been beaten by your house captain. It was not long before I qualified. Discipline was very much in the hands of the boys and flogging by the Headmaster or Lower Master was rare, and I do not recall anyone in my house suffering from either of those two figures. Whereas at Orwell Park the cane had been there but seldom used, only a minority of boys escaped at Eton. The Captain of the House was the nearest person to God and he exercised his authority after consultation with the Housemaster who would almost never question his judgement. In my last half it fell to me to take the place of the Captain of the House, Peter Whiteley, on one occasion when he was ill. A boy had been reported by the boys' maid to the Dame for leaving his room in an exceptionally untidy state. The Dame reported the matter to the Library and I was called upon to inflict punishment. I do remember that I was as lenient as possible, recalling as I did the painful experiences of some four years earlier. The interest from this episode is that the women were anything but sympathetic and a complaint from such a source would not be questioned. It has always surprised me that women who mostly have not experienced corporal punishment tend to be more in favour than men.

While nowadays schools manage their disciplinary problems in a different manner, it would have been a foolish parent or boy who complained in the 1940s. There was a war to win and an Empire to run, and any reaction other than stoicism and obedience would have been met with short shrift. Parents and school governors were aware that boys from public schools were likely soon to be exercising authority, including the administration of justice and punishments, in many different ways all over the world, and it was no bad thing that they should experience both sides of the coin at an early age. While there may have been, as in all forms of justice, cases of abuse, I do not think that the abolition of corporal punishment in schools has been to the benefit of the boys. The only real sanction nowadays for unseemly behaviour is expulsion, and the old system would, I am sure, have prevented the blighting of some school careers and would also have brought some young delinquents to heel in time before they attracted a criminal record.

Another useful experience for the young gentlemen was Early School at 7.30 a.m. (7 a.m. before the First World War). The boys' maid called you at 7 a.m. with hot water which she poured into your wash basin. Early risers were rewarded with a biscuit and cocoa before they left the building for three-quarters of an hour's tuition in a classroom which might be up to a quarter of a mile away. This was abolished some time after the war, more for the benefit of the masters, who hated it, rather than for the benefit of the boys. Once again this was an erosion of a useful discipline for those who came from a more privileged background.

Although there was no long leave (half-term), parents did visit their sons during the war. Celebrations were low key, and in my case my mother came for the 4th of June and my father for St Andrew's Day, usually bringing a pheasant which was then cooked at Rowlands (the school shop) and eaten in one's room for tea. My father used to give me £1 to go back with each half and then five shillings a week. This was almost certainly what his father had done for him and he saw no reason to change such satisfactory arrangements. I was conscious of keeping expenses low and was probably the only boy of my generation to have the same top hat on the day I left as on the day I arrived. I much regret selling it at my auction which all boys had before they left. Despite my frugality my father once wrote to me to say that my bills were too high. They had increased by £2 from the previous half. I did not respond as I did not see what I could do about it. My records reveal that the cost of my education at Eton between 1941 when I arrived and 1946 when I left, including all extras, was £1,434. My education at Orwell Park between 1937 and 1941 had cost £810. The tuition fee at Orwell Park for my last term was £56 and my tuition fee at Eton for my first half was £83.

The war was with us all the time and no one could or would have wished to be unaware of the suffering and the sacrifices. I used to buy the *Eton College Chronicle*, a weekly publication, for onward transmission to my brother in North Africa and to Italy where he was serving with the 12th Lancers from 1943. Each week were recorded the names of the boys who had been killed in action the previous week, which made chilling reading when, as was often the case, it was someone who had left only a year earlier and who had been distinguished in cricket or football. Air-raid warnings were frequent. Each house had its own air-raid shelter and occasionally alarm bells would ring in the middle of the night. When this occurred we had to slip on trousers and a jersey which hung outside our rooms before descending to the shelter to sleep for the remainder of the night on a lilo. As the war progressed and the tide turned in favour of the allies more countries rallied to the cause. The nine o'clock news on Sundays was preceded by the National Anthems of all the countries fighting against Germany. It was a means of raising morale and convincing any doubters, if there were any, that the cause was just. Loyalty to King and Country was on a scale which is unbelievable today. The National Anthem was played at least once during every cinema and theatre performance and everyone stood to attention throughout without question. Not to have done so would have been unacceptable and one would have been rebuked.

During the Easter holidays of 1943 I volunteered to remain at the school for two weeks to undertake air-raid precaution duties. This was to be my only active contribution to the war effort. You had to be 15 years old or more to be accepted and each house was asked to provide at least one volunteer. We were all housed together and had our meals locally. Our responsibilities included watching for fires and looking after people and the school property in the event of an air raid. I believe my period of duty was completely uneventful, but we all much enjoyed ourselves going to the cinema and to Windsor Races, which were activities which were forbidden during the half. It was this duty which brought me together for the first time with Richard Chaloner (subsequently) Gisborough who was to become one of my greatest friends and to whom I would be best man in due course.

Because of limited petrol, activities in the holidays were much restricted, but my father did rent Ardvorlich Moor in Perthshire for the grouse shooting four years running in the

1940s. My father much enjoyed grouse shooting himself but he did this primarily for my brother and me, to give us a early introduction to the sport. I was a participant each year but Julian was an absentee once he had left to join his regiment in North Africa in 1943. With another family we filled the lodge near St Fillans and, subject to the weather, we shot every day for two weeks other than Sundays. There were no beaters and so it was all 'walking up' which is demanding exercise in thick heather in Scotland. The journey by train from Norfolk took over two days each way and we had to go equipped with everything from bicycles to sheets. Climbing the mountain each day to the moor took nearly three-quarters of an hour and apart from the keeper we were assisted by a young man who came with a pony to bring up the lunch and carry down the game. It was a wonderful holiday for me and introduced me to the beauty of Scotland. In Norfolk, where my father had a gun in a syndicate at Cockley Cley, shooting was easier, first because some petrol was allowed for the purpose and second because beaters were available in the form of Italian prisoners of war who were delighted to have a day out.

We were well aware of our good fortune in attending that wonderful school. Games of every description were available and compulsory, and swimming, at a location according to your age, was in the River Thames. For many of us the river was the great escape and we were allowed to row in our 'whiffs' or our 'riggers' as far upstream as our inclination took us. I was always being reminded of my brother's feat in rowing up to Henley, his tutor having arranged for him and his boat to be brought back to the school. The river provided me with one of my great escapes. Exercise of some sort had to be taken, and proved, on a regular basis and a chart was maintained on which you recorded your activities. It was not possible or desirable to participate in a team game every day and one of the alternatives was a run. Running to Locks (Boveney Lock) along the river bank was an accepted piece of exercise. One day in March during my second half I was running to Locks, dribbling a football with Lennox Hannay, when the ball went into the river. The river was uninviting and in spate and as luck would have it the ball had soon drifted to the far bank. To swim and fetch it would have been beyond us, but to return without the ball was equally out of the question. The hour, they say, produces the man, and two very unhappy boys were relieved when another boy, whom we did not know, appeared without a football and also running to Locks. His name was Teddy Gwynne and he was quick to size up both an opportunity and a difficult situation. The fee was 2s 6d each (a useful sum) and it did not take him long to strip down, swim across the fast-flowing river, and return with the football. Everyone was delighted.

In my final year came VE Day on 8 May 1945. The excitement had been growing for weeks, and like everyone else we were delirious with joy. The war in Europe was over; it would only be a matter of time before the whole ghastly business was at an end. We had triumphed in the face of adversity and the standing of our country in Europe and in the world would never be higher. After the defeat of Japan in August the relief was beyond belief. The killing was over and better days would come. As a nation we had achieved so much of which we could be immensely proud.

I obtained five credits and two passes in my examinations for School Certificate which was a fair result for an average boy. I left in March 1946. I had won no prizes but I was an

Upper Boats Cox and won my house colours, and had made many friends, some of whom I see to this day. One of the disadvantages of Eton is that, even though you do not mention it yourself, everyone seems to know you were there and it follows you round for the rest of your life.

CHAPTER 4

I Join the Army
1946-1948

THE WAR WAS OVER. It had been total war and hopefully the last war of its kind. Everyone had been involved and nothing else had mattered except the unconditional surrender of Germany and Japan and this had been achieved, albeit at enormous cost. Besides the loss of life, there had been the blackout and rationing of almost all food other than vegetables. 'Dig for Victory' had been one slogan while another had been 'Don't eat so much bread, eat potatoes instead'. Even sweets were rationed. Some of the allocations were minute: 2 oz of butter per person; 4 oz of margarine and one egg per person per week. This gives some indication of what was on offer. Oranges, lemons and bananas which came from far-away places were non-existent.

There were some notable benefits. First the rationing scheme worked fairly and people were remarkably more healthy than they are today. Obesity was a word which was almost unknown and children's teeth were the better for the lack of sugar and sweets. Perhaps the greatest benefit was the universal determination to put the needs of the country before all others. In 1945 almost everyone who could be was in the services, and the trains were full of people in uniform. HM King George VI wore uniform every day as had his father before him in the previous conflict of 1914-1918.

After two weeks' holiday I joined the army as a private soldier in April 1946. I was instructed to report to Ranby Camp, Retford in Nottinghamshire and was collected from Retford Station. I had been sent a railway warrant and an advance of pay of five shillings (25p) which was deducted from my first week's pay. Pay at that time for a private soldier was three shillings (15p) a day, and on each pay parade I would receive £1. Although I was entitled to twenty-one shillings, one shilling was deducted automatically for barrack damages whether there had been any damages or not. Thus did the army provide for maintenance of its sub-standard property. If I had not joined up voluntarily I would have been conscripted as we were still in what was termed a Duration of Emergency.

Ranby Camp was to be my home for the foreseeable future. Recruits were not allowed out of barracks for the first six weeks of training. On arrival we were each issued with a 'palliasse' which we filled with straw and which would be our bed. We were also issued with everything from a toothbrush upwards as well as two suits of battledress, beret, shirts and every other aspect of uniform. Our new home was a Nissen hut filled with bunks for about forty soldiers. Each bunk had a tiny bed space providing for a locker in which we kept our very few personal possessions. The clothes in which we had arrived were taken from us and posted home: they would no longer be needed as we would not be leaving barracks, and if we did we would go out in uniform.

Training began immediately and we marched everywhere under the direction of two corporals whose every order had to be instantly obeyed. After the issued battledress had been adjusted by the military tailor one pair of trousers was placed between cardboard under a blanket on the palliasse so that you slept on them to keep them pressed. Each person was allocated three blankets. Sheets and pillow-cases were non-existent. Nearly everyone smoked as cigarettes were cheap (one shilling or 5p for twenty) and were one of the few luxuries available. In my barrack room I was one of about five who did not smoke. I always hated it and thought it a complete waste of money.

For the first six weeks we did nothing but drill, weapon-training and attend lectures on current affairs or other basic military activities. We were all assessed by various procedures to determine our potential and in which arm of the service we would serve. The limited spare time we had was spent in the NAAFI where we supplemented our rations, and wrote letters home.

I was unfortunate in that I developed pneumonia and pleurisy before completing my training and was despatched to a military hospital and then to a convalescent home in Halifax. This misfortune put me back by at least six months so that I had to begin the process all over again at Ranby Camp in the autumn. The only advantage was that by the second time round I knew something about it and was joined by some friends from school who had left at the end of the summer. That winter was extraordinarily cold and I remember the snow filtering through the roof of the hut so that each morning those of us on the top tier of the bunk had the added misery of the worst that nature could do. Complaint and any thought of 'rights' was out of the question. Those a little older than us had fought in north-west Europe and service for King and Country was unquestioned. Although it was rough we came to no harm (I had forgotten about my pneumonia by now), and it was a wonderful opportunity for all of us from different backgrounds to mix together and work as a team. We sat at our 'bed spaces' until late at night polishing our boots and making our kit as smart as possible. There were regular inspections by the non-commissioned officers and it was amazing how we were transformed from recruits into presentable soldiers in a few short weeks.

I was earmarked as a potential officer and was transferred to the Royal Military Academy at Sandhurst which had recently reopened as the establishment for training all officers after the war. Up until the outbreak of the Second World War all those earmarked for the infantry and the cavalry were trained at the Royal Military College at Sandhurst whereas those destined for the Royal Artillery and the Royal Engineers were trained at the Royal Military Academy, Woolwich, which was known as 'The Shop'. From now on all regular officers would be trained at the same location.

It was at this time that I put my name forward for a regular commission. There was little choice. The total war had vastly enlarged the armed services, and most of what we would now call the service industries did not exist. Eton had only been interested in Oxford and Cambridge so far as universities were concerned and I was not considered sufficiently academic for a professional career. I do not think anyone ever mentioned the word university to me, and along with so many of my friends I followed what was the obvious alternative. My father had been a regular officer between 1914 and 1932, having served in the Great War with the 5th Lancers from June 1915 until he was wounded at Jussy in March 1918. On the disbandment of the 5th Lancers in 1921 he transferred to the 8th Hussars. It was his suggestion that I join the 16th/5th Lancers and he arranged for me to be interviewed by the then Colonel of the Regiment, Cecil Howard, who himself was the son of a 16th Lancer. At that time regiments were tribal and much liked recruiting sons of former officers. I was somewhat shaken when at my interview at the Cavalry Club, Colonel Howard, in front of my father, said that the fact that my father had served with the 5th Lancers was no guarantee that I would be acceptable. The 16th Lancers had objected to being amalgamated with what they saw as an inferior regiment and Colonel Howard was one of those who did what they could to foster a spirit of antagonism which is beyond comprehension today. He also asked me what pack of hounds I hunted with, almost certainly knowing that I came from Norfolk where hunting was low key and had not included me. It was an inauspicious start, and I was somewhat surprised that hunting should be so high on the agenda when we had so recently survived the greatest conflict the world had ever seen.

   I joined Intake 1A at Sandhurst on 2 May 1947 and, while life was more civilized, I found the curriculum to be almost as restricting as at Ranby Camp. Concentration was on drill, weapon-training and a number of military activities in which I was not really interested. Perhaps I was not meant to be a soldier after all. It did not really matter, as I had been brought up in the expectation of joining my father in the family brewery in Norwich. No one had ever considered whether it was either desirable or possible for both my brother and me to be employed in the brewery, but in retrospect, it is now obvious that there would not have been room for both of us. My father never did discuss the matter with my brother and me. Joining the army to gain experience was what many young people did before embarking on a different career.

It was while I was at Sandhurst that I developed my passion for backing horses which was to affect my whole life. I had begun to follow racing in a small way before I left Eton and I used to accompany my father to almost every race meeting at Newmarket which in those days was restricted to the spring and autumn fixtures on the Rowley Mile and the summer meeting on the July course. There were no weekend or evening fixtures in those days. Admission to the club was then restricted to those whose vouchers were signed by a Member of the Jockey Club. My father did not arrange this and so I was restricted to Tattersalls, but joined him and my step-mother between races. A young mind can absorb quantities of information and I quickly learned the rudiments of what is a very complicated industry. Backing horses for most people is fun, and so it was for me, but I also turned it into a business. Racing had been kept going in a small way during the war on a limited number of racecourses. Like everything else, racing was slow to recover and the number of horses in training and the number of fixtures were far removed from what applies today. This meant that there were fewer owners and trainers and the fields tended to be small. A small number of prominent owners and trainers dominated the sport and finding winners was much easier than it is today. Betting tax was not introduced until 1966 and until about 1950 the Tote paid a place dividend on the first three in any race where there were at least seven runners as opposed to the eight runners which applies today. In addition the Tote guaranteed a minimum dividend of one penny on a two shilling stake whatever the odds. I have often done things differently to other people and I developed my own method for backing horses which, while it suited me, was against all the recognized rules of gambling. I backed hot favourites and often for a place only at the Tote return. The returns were often much better than what would have been anticipated.

The reason I indulged in backing horses was because I needed money to do the things I wanted with my friends. When I had been 16 my father had given me an allowance of £10 a quarter, or £40 a year, which was paid into my Barclays Bank account and which was all I had to meet all normal expenditure. This was probably somewhat less than was available to my contemporaries, but the allowance had increased to £100 a year by the time I reached Sandhurst where, of course, I also received my army pay. It is when you are young that you need money for all sorts of reasons, and my calculating mind told me that I could increase my income by judicious investment at the races. And so it had begun, with the opening of credit accounts with the Sandhurst bookmaker, Mr Mack, and also accounts with Tote Investors as they were then and Ladbroke & Co. It was, as I say, a business and all bets were faithfully recorded in my betting book. The average stake at that time was £10 which would be approximately £200 today. Many of us studied the racing pages of the newspapers but I do not think anyone else took it as seriously as I did. I also opened an account with William Hill, who almost immediately closed it, sending a registered letter saying, 'The type of business you bring is of no value to the firm'!

The result was that I learned a great deal very quickly, and I did manage to make money. Many years later I was to say to Sir Desmond Plummer when he became Chairman of the Levy Board that betting was like sex: no one could teach you and you had to discover for yourself. I think he appreciated the analogy.

One of the features of Sandhurst at that time was the standard of officers who were our instructors. Almost all had been especially chosen by their regiments and had had distinguished service or won decorations for gallantry. At least two had two DSOs and three MCs. Besides acting as instructors they were there to recruit officers for their own regiments. We were told that we were the cream of the nation's youth and we had to work hard to be sure of a commission in the regiment of our choice. Drill seemed to be never ending and there was extra drill for the slightest misdemeanour. My course ended with the customary Passing Out Parade on 20 October 1948 and I passed out number 132 out of 260 cadets. I was no star but I felt respectable.

CHAPTER 5

My Commissioned Service
1948-1961

I WAS COMMISSIONED on 26 November 1948, into the 16th/5th Lancers who had moved to Camp 53, Fanara, near Fayid in the Canal Zone of Egypt. The regiment was equipped with Daimler armoured cars which had had an impressive record in the Western Desert during the Second World War. The regiment was in the Canal Zone to be available to honour treaty rights with Egypt in the event of an incursion by Israeli troops into Egyptian territory.

I sailed from Liverpool on board the troopship *El Nil* to arrive at Port Said and eventually my regiment on Christmas Day 1948. It was not a good day to arrive but a more experienced officer named Peter Holland managed to secure a vehicle to take us the 70 miles from Port Said to Fayid. Nobody particularly wanted to welcome a new officer on Christmas Day and my morale was at rock bottom when I was shown to a tent with little more than a bed, a chair and a table. Furniture had to be acquired over a period of time as other officers left and to begin with I lived out of my tin trunk and a suitcase.

There was no running water except for a shower and the privy was a deep hole in the ground. Any creature comforts, and they were few, were confined to the Officers' Mess. I was pleased to discover that there was a good supply of newspapers which included air mail editions of *The Times* (then almost essential reading for anyone calling themselves educated) and the *Sporting Life*. I was able to follow my interest in racing. Before departure I had arranged with Ladbroke & Co. that I would have £5 to win on every horse which had a returned starting price of evens. My theory was that more horses won at evens than lost, and this seemed to me to be the only way I could participate in my hobby; accounts were to be settled monthly. After six months I stopped it and I recall I was a loser by £10. Letters from home were vital and I continued my practice of writing weekly to my mother and father.

It was not long before I was caught up in events. Much time was spent on exercises in the desert when we would be away from camp for ten days at a time. It was hot by day and cold by night and even more uncomfortable. The very limited water supply meant that eating utensils had to be rubbed clean with sand and the days seemed interminably long. It was during my second exercise, within three months of joining, that I was told my tent had been burned down. I had lost everything except what I had with me. It transpired that my batman (soldier servant), in my absence, had been having a siesta on my bed and had thrown his cigarette away which then set the tent alight. The army ordered a Court of Enquiry which resulted in the soldier being found guilty of some offence and being ordered to pay ten shillings towards the cost of the tent! Fortunately my insurance company made good my financial loss but clothes made locally hardly measured up to those supplied by the regimental tailor.

Young officers seemed to be particularly vulnerable to misfortune. No one warned us about possible disasters. I was followed a few months later by one James Holmpatrick whom I had known at Eton. His father had died and he had inherited the Irish peerage. He was reputed to be broke but nevertheless his trunks and equipment were clearly marked in large letters Lord Holmpatrick. Within a few weeks of arrival most of his smart clothes and other personal possessions had been stolen: removed from his tent in the middle of the night. Theft was a problem for all ranks and the culprits were invariably local Egyptian boys. In this case, even if they could not read, they knew what a Lord was and most Lords had money. Eventually the trail led to the Head Syce (Stablehand) but he was far too valuable to be sacked, and James, like me, had to start again.

In another respect I was more fortunate. The army always encouraged officers to participate in every conceivable sporting activity. I had brought my gun with me from home and this was stored in the regimental armoury. I received an invitation from a school friend, David Keown-Boyd, who had heard I had arrived in Egypt, to stay with his family in their palatial house in Cairo. The invitation was to shoot duck on the British Ambassador's shoot at Tel el Kebir. This was considered to be a rare privilege as the other officers were lucky to be offered a day on the army shoot which was nothing like so good. The British at that time still had influence in Egypt and David's father had some position in the Egyptian government. The arrangements were splendid. We were taken to a village in the evening before the shoot where the accommodation, even if it was in a tent, was quite different from Camp 53. Servants of every kind made sure that every comfort was provided, and a magnificent breakfast preceded the day's sport. There were forty guns and each gun was given two Egyptian boys to carry equipment and to transport him to his butt which was situated somewhere in the lake. At 8 a.m. His Excellency the Ambassador, Sir

Ronald Campbell, fired two shots into the air. This was the signal to the guns that shooting could begin, and to the duck that they had to fly. Fly they did, over a vast expanse of water and shooting continued until 12 noon. The forty guns were all far apart so there was no danger to each other, and the two boys would swim around retrieving whatever was shot. If you did not get enough they would probably retrieve some from somebody else so that everyone managed a respectable score. My neighbour was one Giles Bey who was Chief of Police in Cairo and who had his cartridges specially sent from New York and he, of course, was the main contributor to the bag. I cannot remember the details but several hundred duck would have been shot each day. Earlier in the season the Duke of Edinburgh had been a guest and the bag had been over a thousand. I would not want to do it now, but then it seemed the greatest fun. Each boy was rewarded with 50 piastres, then the equivalent of ten shillings.

Other activities included riding in the desert and swimming in the Great Bitter Lake. I once swam the Suez Canal so that I could say I had set foot in Sinai. This was extremely foolish as I had to judge the moment between ships and there was a strong current, of which I was unaware, which carried me a long way from my point of departure. I was relieved to be back and did not wish to do it again.

We endured the inevitable 'khamsins' which would blow for days at a time and resulted in sand penetrating every garment and even covering one's toothbrush.

Approximately once every three weeks one was Orderly Officer with responsibility for inspecting the guard and visiting the sentries at night. It was my misfortune to be awakened one night in the early hours to be told that there had been a serious accident. On arriving at the scene I discovered that a soldier who was one of the guards had gone to the vehicle park and collected a half-track (a special type of armoured car) and driven it intentionally at the Dhobi's tent (laundry) and run him over and killed him. It transpired that the soldier, Trooper Van Royan, had been angry because the Dhobi had not cleaned his equipment sufficiently well for him to be awarded 'the stick man' which would have excused him guard duty for the night. I had done the inspection before the guard went on duty and had obviously selected someone else! Because Van Royan was of South African extraction he had certain views which resulted in this awful fatality. He was, of course, tried and convicted of manslaughter and sentenced to life imprisonment, but he was returned to South Africa and eventually only served about four years. This was the only occasion when I was to be a witness at a major trial.

Entertainment in the evenings was scarce. There were no cars and no girls. Who would put up with it today? The only females were a few officers' wives who had married quarters adjacent to the Great Bitter Lake and they generously entertained us to dinner, and this at least was a break from the interminable evenings in the Officers' Mess where we played poker, bezique and piquet. We had to change for dinner every evening. One's batman laid out one's clothes and a trumpeter played 'Officers Dress' at 7 p.m. daily. Each regiment had its own band and there were trumpet calls throughout the day from Reveille in the morning to Last Post at night. Mess kit was worn, except that on Wednesdays and Saturdays one could book out (if there was anywhere to go), and those who were in wore a dinner jacket. Sunday was even more relaxed and one could wear a suit. An open-neck shirt or a cardigan would have been impossible. Standards were maintained as in the previous hundred years.

Once every six weeks there was a guest night and these were special occasions when the regiment entertained local dignitaries. Regiments like the 16th/5th Lancers had an array of fine silver and crested china, and they were all able to put on a fine show and entertain lavishly. On one such occasion I had one of my most fortunate escapes. The usual gathering of local grandees was present including the General Officer Commanding British Troops in Egypt, the Brigadier, the District Commissioner, and others who considered themselves close to the Almighty. A wonderful dinner had been enjoyed with the band playing and we had got as far as the brandy, when one of the mess waiters appeared offering everyone a cigar. I, as a non-smoker, refused, but my neighbour said 'Come on Martin, have a cigar and enjoy yourself'. My father had smoked a cigar every night of his life and I enjoyed the smell, but he had never warned me of any effects. I took a cigar and had hardly lit up when suddenly the whole room started going round in circles in my head. I guessed what was going to happen and rushed out and just managed to get to the lavatory in time. It was a very near thing and it was lucky that as a very junior officer I was sitting at the end of the table near the exit so nobody noticed my departure. Had I been at the other end of the table my whole history might have been different.

In April 1950 the regiment moved to Barce, some 65 miles inland from Benghazi in Cyrenaica. I was delighted to exchange a tented camp in the desert for proper barracks in a more attractive part of North Africa. The regiment had a new Commanding Officer, Douglas Kaye, who had been awarded the DSO and bar with the 10th Hussars, and he and his wife, Audrey, were to become life-long friends. It was while we were in Barce that I nearly drowned. We were swimming at Tocra when I and Tony Wootton and John Davies were caught in a freak Mediterranean storm. We were slightly out of our depth but in sight of our friends on the shore when, without warning, a tornado turned the sea into a cauldron of rough water. I was slightly out beyond the others but we all realized we had to swim for the shore and it was undoubtedly a case of *'sauve qui peut'*. I was the weakest swimmer and soon realized I was not only making no progress but was actually being carried out to sea. There was no hope, but instinct makes one carry on. I thought I would never see anyone again and my mind covered all the things which would naturally come to anyone in a similar situation, but I kept on swimming and began swallowing salt water. The experience probably lasted no more than a quarter of an hour, and then suddenly the storm subsided as swiftly as it had begun and I found, to my amazement, that I was being carried by another current back towards the shore where I was washed up in an exhausted condition. After time for recovery and prayers of thankfulness for my release I began walking up the beach in the direction of where my friends were likely to be. There was a happy reunion when I found them with some locals who had gathered ropes and were looking for me in deep water where I had last been seen. Since then I have hardly ventured out of my depth and certainly not in foreign waters. Unfortunately one or two soldiers did drown and I have no doubt that precautions have been improved since those rather carefree days.

In 1952 the regiment converted to Comet Tanks as a Divisional Regiment, Royal Armoured Corps, and moved to

Zavia near Tripoli where one squadron was stationed in Gialo Barracks, and this was to be our final station in the Middle East before returning in 1953 for a short spell in England for the Coronation. After the Coronation we became an armoured regiment with Centurion tanks and moved to Athlone Barracks in Sennelager where we became part of the British Army of the Rhine. While we were at Sennelager I was able to do some serious race riding. I had bought a mare called Clivia from an officer in the 9th Lancers and she provided me with several opportunities to ride in both chases and hurdle races, but I was never better than third. I also developed my skill as a 'croupier' after visiting a number of casinos in Belgium, France and Germany and this was to add to the enjoyment of regimental guest nights where roulette had become a feature of entertainment.

My father died in 1955. He was ten days short of his 61st birthday but had been ill for the previous two years. My brother and I were told that one of us must leave the army at once to join the family firm in Norwich. It was, of course, too late as one of us should have been involved much earlier. My brother was a Staff Officer in Corps Headquarters in Germany but had been married the year before and his wife was expecting Emma, their first child. He was released from the army and became an employee of Youngs, Crawshay & Youngs Ltd. Within twelve months the firm was to be bought by Bullard and Sons, another Norwich brewery. There was no way the company could have resisted the bid, and the two firms had had an exchange of directors since 1941. My father had told me before he died that we would be unable to continue to operate independently indefinitely. All four Norwich breweries had had an agreement to assist each other

Escorting Her Majesty the Queen during the inspection of the Oxford University Air Squadron, 4 November 1960.

in the event of a bomb attack during the Second World War, and this agreement had been effective following the direct hit on Morgans Brewery. All four breweries would in due course become part of Watneys and eventually brewing would cease in Norwich altogether. The family did, of course, do well financially under the deal and recovered some of the money which had been paid in death duty the previous year. Julian remained employed by both Bullards and Watneys until that firm was bought by Grand Metropolitan in 1974.

It was in 1955 that I was appointed Adjutant of my regiment and I was very pleased at what I saw as confidence in my ability. I had been warned that being Adjutant would be demanding and involve long hours of dedication. I was fortunate to be working with Anthony Bullivant, a most able commanding officer, and to be assisted by a long-serving Regimental Sergeant Major (RSM W.C. Marshall DCM) who had held the post since before I joined and who knew everything about regimental organization. I was also fortunate in that I had two able assistants in Michael Price and David McLeod who undertook all the tasks which I did not like.

There followed two happy years before we returned to Catterick to become a training regiment. I had ceased to be Adjutant and handed that responsibility over to John Pownall. On 19 March 1959 the regiment paraded at Buckingham Palace when Her Majesty the Queen presented a Guidon in recognition of the bicentenary of the formation of the 16th The Queen's Lancers. I commanded No. 2 Guard on the parade and was responsible for engaging the artist William Dring who painted a picture to commemorate the occasion. The parade was followed by a dinner and a ball at the Hyde Park Hotel which was attended by Her Majesty.

It was while we were at Catterick that I concluded that I did not want to remain in the army. The thought of returning once more to BAOR with endless exercises did not appeal. Armoured regiments did not any longer go to interesting places. People did not like tanks pounding around the countryside and regimental life was becoming less satisfying. The Staff College exam lay ahead and I knew I would have to retire before my superiors discovered my weaknesses. However, I was to enjoy one more posting when I went for two years as Adjutant to the Oxford University Officers' Training Corps in 1959. This was a wonderful end to my military service: I felt privileged to be associated with academic life and I was fortunate to be invited to dine in some of the colleges. The offices in Manor Road were staffed by civilians and my job was to assist in recruiting undergraduates which I did with enthusiasm. We arranged a summer camp on Salisbury Plain and most of those associated with the OTC were helpful and friendly. I was even given a house to live in despite misgivings on the part of certain people who thought that, as a bachelor, I would turn it into a den of iniquity. The highlight of this secondment was the visit of Her Majesty the Queen on 4 November 1960 when she inspected the OTC and the University Air Squadron. Her Majesty's first remark to me was 'What are you doing here?' This was because she had been Colonel-in-Chief of my regiment since 1947 and, being well briefed, she knew that I was one of her officers.

In early 1961 I left the army. I had had nearly fifteen years' varied and enjoyable service, but I knew I had reached my ceiling. I had made many good friends and I had been best man to four of my brother officers, namely Richard Gisborough, John Pownall, Michael Price and Christopher Robinson. My service was insufficient to qualify for a pension but I received a gratuity of £2,000 which was a useful contribution towards the cost of my first house. What was I to do now?

CHAPTER 6

Betwixt and Between
1961-1963

I KNEW WHEN I LEFT the army that finding the right opening for me was not going to be easy. I had no qualifications and I was 33. I was totally absorbed by racing and I registered my name with Weatherbys, the Secretaries to the Jockey Club, in the hope of employment as an official such as Clerk of the Course, Starter or Handicapper. At that time any one of those jobs would have suited me admirably as they would have forced me to give up betting and the idea of working on the racecourse appealed very much. I was told how few jobs there were but that I would be advised if an opportunity occurred. Most racing officials at that time, and for several years afterwards, were ex-officers who had some sort of experience in regiments like mine. I lived in hope, but I knew I had to avoid wasting time.

While I had been in the army, everything had been provided, and even at the Oxford University OTC I had a bicycle allowance and an allowance towards the cost of a 'maid' who looked after my house and managed my laundry. Following my father's death I had certain possessions and I recognized the need for a house of my own.

I have had many lucky breaks and I had recently walked into one of the luckiest of all. In November 1960 I had been lunching in the Cavalry Club (as it then was) when, by chance, I met a friend called David Wade who was several years younger than me and whom I had met as a National Service officer when he was at Catterick. After exchanging the usual greetings he asked me what I was doing, and I replied that I was looking for a house. At that point of time I had not actually made any enquiries or looked at anything. He replied at once 'I have the house for you: come with me in my car and we will go there now'. At that time parking was no problem and so together we went to what was to become my home for the next nine years, 117 Dovehouse Street in Chelsea. The house was at the Fulham Road end of the street and was one of three which had recently been completed. Decorating had not been done and the garden, which was approximately 20 ft by 12 ft had not been begun.

As soon as I walked in, without a moment's hesitation, I knew that this was the house for me. It had a drawing-room, a dining-room, three bedrooms, two bathrooms and a basement area. It was ideal in every way and I immediately wrote to the agents offering them the asking price of £15,500 for a 63-year lease which was accepted. I was quite delighted and no one can ever have bought a house so quickly and with so little trouble. Over the next two months, with much help from my mother, I completed the decoration and was able to move in.

I was enormously grateful to David Wade. I have often thought how few people would give the time to do what he did for me, and what a chance it was that we met when we did. The house was to give me great pleasure.

One piece of luck was followed by another. I immediately advertised for a housekeeper and this yielded one called Hilda Martin who came to me and worked first for me and then for Grania and me until she died. We always called her Miss Martin and I cannot think why I never got round to calling her Hilda. Hilda was one of the old school who had been in service all her life and had recently worked for a gentleman in the Albany. Although I did not realize it at the time, she was interviewing me. Hilda was already approaching 60, but the house suited her well and she was willing to do breakfast for guests and the occasional dinner party for me. The arrangement was ideal.

Good fortune was followed by real tragedy. I decided to give my first dinner party and invited established friends, the most important of whom was David Wade who had found me my house. Acceptances arrived, but I heard no word from David. Eventually, I telephoned his home in East Yorkshire only to be told that he had been killed in a car accident. I was devastated that I was never able to show him what he had done for me and I really did owe him more than I could ever repay.

My friends descended like locusts. The visitors' book records an endless flow of young marrieds and others who were only too pleased to take advantage of a bachelor's house in a fashionable part of London before they had accommodation of their own. I, for my part, was equally pleased that they did come so that I could repay much hospitality which I had had over the years staying with them in the country. Although I did not know it at the time my future wife used to walk past my front door every day on her way to Faulkner House in Brechin Place where she was a secretary.

I had to have some form of employment and my cousin William introduced me to one of his friends who worked for a firm of stockbrokers called Roger Mortimer & Company, and so I became attached to them. I knew on arrival it would not last. There were people younger than me who already had years of experience and I would never be able to catch up. I was with them for thirteen months, and as you learn more in your first year in any job it was not a waste of time. I learned how the Stock Exchange worked, and when I eventually joined the Horserace Betting Levy Board they thought (quite wrongly of course) that I must know all about money. As the payments from the levy on bookmakers began to flow in I was not unduly surprised when they asked me for an introduction to the City. I put them in touch with Cazenoves and this was to be to the advantage of both sides.

Work was not too onerous and I spent most weekends away from London. I shall always be grateful to the many people who had me to stay over and over again, and particular mention has to be made of my brother and sister-in-law, Julian and Ann, William and Elisabeth Crawshay who then lived at Llanfair Court near Abergavenny which has now been passed on to Huw and Philippa Crawshay, Lennox Hannay with his lovely house at Spring Hill near Moreton-in-Marsh, John and Ginny Goldsmid and Richard and Shane Gisborough who always entertained regally at the converted stables at Gisborough Hall.

I knew that I had to find a permanent job to which I was really suited and I kept on with my enquiries with Weatherbys. Racing jobs come at unexpected moments and you have to be available when the opportunity occurs. I widened my enquiries and visited the Officers' Association which specializes in finding employment for ex-officers from the armed services. I looked at the list of opportunities which were displayed and found most of them to be uninspiring. However, when I was called for interview a piece of paper was produced from inside a desk which had not been on general offer, and this was the opportunity for a post at the Horserace Betting Levy Board which had been established by the Government in September 1961. As soon as I read the piece of paper I knew that this was exactly what I wanted and I was delighted when the Association arranged for me to be interviewed at the Board's offices in Euston Road. Most of us had been brought up not to expect to get what we want, but I really wanted this job and I was overwhelmed with happiness when, shortly after two interviews, I received a letter from the Board's Secretary, Major-General Sir Rupert Brazier-Creagh, offering me an appointment as Deputy Assistant Secretary at a salary of £1,250 a year. I accepted with alacrity and handed in my notice to Roger Mortimer & Co. I would now be properly employed in an industry in which I was passionately interested and where I felt I had something to offer. Life depends on luck and it was lucky for me that the Officers' Association had that job just on the day I called. The Levy Board would not publicly advertise another executive position for over twenty years.

CHAPTER 7

The Horserace Betting Levy Board – Inception
1963

I JOINED THE Horserace Betting Levy Board on 25 March 1963. The Board was unique in that it was the only national organization outside the Government with the power to raise and distribute money for a particular purpose. It was established in 1961 with all-party support as a Statutory Board under the Home Office, and was charged with the responsibility of collecting monetary contributions from both the bookmakers and the Horserace Totalisator Board and applying them, towards the improvement of breeds of horses, the advancement or encouragement of veterinary science or veterinary education, and the improvement of horseracing. Whereas the Tote, which was also a Statutory Board under the Home Office had, since inception as the Racecourse Betting Control Board in 1928, made contributions to racing, the amount contributed by bookmakers to the industry from which they derived their principal livelihood had been limited to a small number of voluntary donations.

I was immensely excited about my new job which appeared to comprise everything in which I was interested; racing, money, people and horses. I caught the Number 14 bus each morning in the Fulham Road which took me all the way to the Board's offices which had been established above the Horserace Totalisator Board at 163 Euston Road. The staff at that time numbered approximately thirty, including some five executives, a commissionaire supplied by the Royal Artillery Association who had served in the First World War and a tea lady. Nearly all the senior staff had military backgrounds and about half were responsible for collecting the levy. Although the Board had been established for over a year, the distribution process had hardly begun as money could not be made available before it was collected.

One of the executives was responsible for the collection of the levy and the remainder, under the Secretary, later to become, as in all organizations, the Chief Executive, were responsible for the more interesting activity, that of spending. I was the last executive to be appointed for the original group, and the reason for my appointment was first, because the Board had taken over responsibility for the National Stud from the Ministry of Agriculture and second, because my immediate superior, Brigadier Oliver Brooke, who had distinguished service with the Welch Regiment in the Second World War, had decided to work only two days a week. I was given particular responsibility for the grants to the horse and pony societies and was made Secretary of the Veterinary Advisory Committee, which was responsible to the Board for the grants to veterinary science and veterinary education, and Secretary of the National Stud Committee. Thus began my long love affair with the world of equine vets which has been so beneficial to me and which continues to this day. I also assisted with prize money grants and improvements to racecourses which were to absorb most of the Board's expenditure for years to come.

It was not long before I discovered my good fortune to be responsible for the Board's administration of what I subsequently termed the 'fringe activities', which also included grants to farriery, point-to-points and racing charities. These were all interesting and brought me into contact with many people who were not directly concerned with horseracing and who mostly knew very little about it.

The first Secretary of the Levy Board, who had interviewed me and who was responsible for establishing the Board, was Major-General Sir Rupert Brazier-Creagh who was another with a distinguished military career, and with the unusual distinction of having been knighted as a Major-General and who, in his capacity of Director of Staff Duties at the War Office had been responsible for the air lift of forces to Kuwait in 1960. He surprised me in particular in two ways, first, by saying that he had loathed the army and second because he was not a member of a Service Club which was most unusual for someone of his seniority at that time. He was passionate about his interest in horseracing, was the owner of a small stud in Ireland, and was an ardent Tote monopolist.

Although it was a small organization the Board had prepared proper terms and conditions of service covering everything from holidays to rules on betting. The rules on betting stipulated that cash betting was permitted but credit accounts were strictly forbidden. This did not suit me as, still a bachelor, I much enjoyed betting and this was how I maintained my knowledge of what was going on in the industry. It has always been recognized that those associated with the running of a race could not be allowed to bet, and persons such as jockeys, starters, handicappers and similar officials accept this from the outset.

I realized that those members of the Levy Board staff who were responsible for collecting the levy could not be allowed to bet on credit to avoid any possible implication with bookmakers, but I did not see why the rule should apply to me who had no such contact. This theory of mine was to be fully vindicated in a few years time when George Wigg became Chairman and frequently telephoned Ladbrokes from his office. I, therefore, made my own rule and carried on as before without, of course, saying a word to anyone. It was at about this time that the well-known bookmakers, Laurie Wallis, told me 'The Levy does not touch us'. It was a pity that some of the Board members were not sufficiently aware of the true situation, or if they were, did so little about it.

My work at the Levy Board enabled me to go racing on a regular basis and I still enjoyed considerable success as a punter, to such an extent that I very occasionally helped others. On one such occasion I escorted a young lady, of whom I was particularly fond, to Sandown Park and was dismayed to discover that she owed her bookmaker £40 which she would have difficulty in paying. I was delighted to help her by backing a favourite to meet her loss and credit her account if the horse won, while the bet would be transferred to me if the horse lost. The horse did win and a happy girl-friend appreciated my flair.

The Board was composed of distinguished people and, apart from the Chairman and two other members who were appointed by the Home Secretary, were well known on the racecourse.

The first Chairman was Field Marshal Lord Harding of Petherton who had been appointed by Mr R.A. Butler who was Home Secretary at the time. Lord Harding had served in the First World War, had been a Divisional Commander in the Second World War, had commanded the British Army of the Rhine after the war and had been Chief of the Imperial General Staff between 1952 and 1955. He had subsequently been Commander-in-Chief in Cyprus where he had locked up Archbishop Makarios who was held responsible for terrorist action on the island at that time. He also held numerous directorships and was Deputy Chairman of Plessey, the electronics firm, and was an ADC to HM King George VI and to HM The Queen. No one could have had a finer career and he was much admired by everyone who knew him. His credentials were impeccable and he should have had the ability which was required, and in particular he should have been able to exert authority over the Bookmakers.

People were to say to me how lucky I was to work under John Harding, and in some ways they were right, but you never know reality until a crisis occurs and the chips are down. Lord Harding used to visit the Board's offices two days a week, and his weakness was that he knew very little about racing and was very much under the control of Rupert Brazier-Creagh who, as I have already indicated, did know his subject well. I was always surprised how much Rupert knew about racing, bearing in mind his distinguished military career which had kept him overseas for so much of his life. It was soon apparent to me that it was a great weakness that the Chairman was so much under the influence of his chief staff officer. The other great weakness of Lord Harding was that he was ill at ease with the grandees of the Jockey Club who still held sway at that time and who, while much welcoming the establishment of the Levy, were reluctant to see the power of expenditure, without which racing could not survive, in hands other than their own. People like the Duke of Norfolk, Lord Rosebery and Lord

Sefton had been pillars of the Turf establishment for years and were used to controlling every aspect of horseracing.

The Board was established some sixteen years after the end of the Second World War and it is, therefore, not surprising that, as with many similar organizations, there was still a preponderance of military figures. This was still a time when there was a sharp division between Board and staff and the breakdown of the class barriers had not yet begun. It was not surprising that the bookmakers addressed Lord Harding as 'you and your military junta'.

This was the organization which I had joined and it was not going to be long before I was disillusioned. Perhaps I should have been surprised that an organization such as the Board should have allowed one of its executives, Oliver Brooke, to become part-time to suit his own convenience. That Lord Harding and the Board could accept such a proposal even then seemed extraordinary.

CHAPTER 8

The Horserace Betting Levy Board – Dismissal
1966

MY FIRST TASK on arrival was to make the annual payment to the Equine Research Station of the Animal Health Trust and the grants which had already been approved to the various horse and pony societies. I made it my business to ensure that all grants approved by the Board were paid on 1 April each year so that recipients, who had already been informed, received their money at the earliest possible time. This was immensely popular and made it easier for those concerned to plan ahead. Some grants had been paid by the old Tote Charity Trust (whose distributive function had now been superseded), but there was a general complaint that no one ever knew when the money would be forthcoming. I was anxious that the Board should have as many friends as possible, and this new initiative, which prevailed throughout my service, was advantageous to those concerned and eliminated bureaucracy. The Board's Veterinary Advisory Committee of which I was Secretary, under the Chairmanship of Sir John Ritchie, a previous Chief Veterinary Officer at the Ministry of Agriculture, were soon in business. The Tote had made some small veterinary grants in the past but nothing had been done on a regular basis; equine research was starved of financial support and very little work in any discipline was being undertaken. The horse was not considered to be an agricultural animal and no government money was available for horse work in the veterinary schools in universities. This was to be changed dramatically and, largely because of the Board's investment, real progress would be made over the next thirty years which would enable future equine specialists to become world leaders in their particular discipline.

The first task, however, was to provide for units where research work could be undertaken, and the first grants were of £5,000 each in 1963 to the Equine Research Station in Newmarket and to each of the six veterinary schools, to provide for buildings, stabling and equipment. These initial grants were almost immediately doubled and £10,000 did, at that time, provide for a reasonable building or stable.

I was lucky to be the most recently appointed executive and I was fortunate to be given responsibility for what, at the time, appeared to be the less glamorous activities. My more senior colleagues were inundated with requests for help from racecourses and busy with the preparation of a prize money scheme, and the needs of the likes of Ascot and Newmarket received the direct attention of the Board while I was able to attend, with virtually no interference, to the fringe activities. It was not long before I realized that the smaller the grant the greater the need. I also discovered that, apart from Rupert Brazier-Creagh, I was the only executive who had any real knowledge of racing and how it worked. My friends all thought I was so lucky, as indeed I was, to have landed a job which might have been made for me. The fact that my colleagues were without much racecourse experience meant that they all thought I knew more than I did. This is a very useful advantage in any industry.

Rupert Brazier-Creagh was a brilliant staff officer and

deserves great credit for establishing the Board and introducing the appropriate mechanism for collection of the levy. It is a point of interest that the first year was the only year in which the contribution from the Tote exceeded the contribution from the bookmakers. He was a good man to work for and my first eighteen months were as enjoyable as I could have hoped for. Since you spend nearly half the day at work it is important to enjoy what you do; if you do not enjoy your job you are almost certainly doing the wrong thing.

The Board's staff problems began in July 1964 with the appointment of a Colonel Paddy Victory in August 1964 to replace Oliver Brooke who had finally fully retired because of ill-health. This was the first of many staff surprises and the first of a whole series of appointments of 'personal friends' to jobs in a statutory board which should have been open to public competition. It was particularly surprising because Rupert Brazier-Creagh had already given the matter his consideration as is shown by the following letter which was sent to all racecourses, and signed by him, on 27 January, 1964:

> I have to inform you that owing to ill-health Brigadier O.G. Brooke, Assistant Secretary, has unfortunately been forced to tender his resignation from the Staff of the Levy Board.
>
> In future matters which were previously referred to Brigadier Brooke will be dealt with by Mr M.R.C. Crawshay, Deputy Assistant Secretary.

Paddy Victory was a friend of Rupert's who had the unusual distinction of having to leave the army following a mutiny in his regiment in Kenya. Although he had commanded a Royal Horse Artillery regiment he was not remotely interested in racing. His qualification was that he was quick to learn and was a first-class writer of papers. I realized, since he and I were to share an office, that there was a real danger of his taking over my work and I was convinced there was no need for his appointment. The letter to all racecourses of January 1964 had already indicated that no replacement was necessary for Oliver Brooke and nothing had changed since then. How could Lord Harding have agreed to such an extraordinary appointment?

The entire racing industry was surprised when in early summer 1965 Rupert Brazier-Creagh resigned the Secretaryship of the Levy Board. He was only 55 and was giving up what could be considered to be the most important administrative job in racing. He was a powerful man in a powerful position and he knew he was helping to shape the future of the industry. Even more amazing was the discovery that the reason for his departure was that he had been given an ultimatum. It had been discovered that besides being Secretary of the Board he had taken a paid position as Manager of the Ardenode Stud in Ireland on behalf of Mrs Meg Mullion. Apart from the fact that he would not have had time to do both jobs it was totally wrong for him to accept a position in the private sector when he was already in a key position in the public sector which, in due course, would have led to a conflict of interest. Lord Harding did not confront Rupert himself but instructed the head of the Board's public relations firm at the time, a Mr Pat Dolan, to meet him and arrange for him to resign from one position or the other. Rupert, to my amazement, decided to resign from the Board and stay as Manager of the Ardenode Stud, but within three months he had fallen out with Paddy Prendergast, Mrs Mullion's trainer, and so achieved the almost impossible feat of losing two key jobs in quick succession. This then was the reason why he had arranged for the appointment of Paddy Victory as an Assistant Secretary to the Board, so that he could write papers and assist with the Board's administration while he, Rupert, visited Ireland to fulfil his obligations to the Ardenode Stud. It is hard to imagine how Rupert thought he would get away with it, and what a shock it must have been to Lord Harding to be let down by the man on whom he relied so much. This was to have major implications for me, and was also a colossal indictment of the Board's supervision of its staff.

There was one other Assistant Secretary besides Paddy Victory and his name was Bernard Catchpole. He had served in the Colonial Service and had been an applicant for the Secretaryship and was taken on by Rupert Brazier-Creagh when the first members of staff were appointed. He had no knowledge of racing and was clearly unsuitable for the Secretaryship which was now to become vacant. For reasons that are already obvious, Paddy Victory, the other Assistant Secretary, was also unsuitable, and so it was decided to advertise the vacancy in the national press. I was then 37 and was not likely to be promoted over the two Assistant Secretaries, even though I knew that I had made a very favourable impact since my appointment two years previously. While Rupert had been there I knew that my job was safe since he had appointed me and we had got on extremely well. I realized that a new person was bound to find out immediately that the Board was overstaffed and that the consequences could be unpleasant and far reaching. Overstaffing is always more serious than understaffing.

I had an interview with Rupert on 11 June to represent to

him my anxieties over his replacement and the effect this would have on the existing staff. Rupert recognized the problem and suggested that I should see Lord Harding to make the same points to him. I therefore saw Lord Harding in the Board Room on 15 June and made it clear to him that we already had too many executives and that the problem would be exacerbated by bringing in someone new from outside. It was, of course, Lord Harding's fault that he had allowed the overstaffing to occur in the first place, and he had also accepted the appointment of Rupert's personal friend as Assistant Secretary to a post that had never been advertised. I was extremely pleased that Lord Harding was grateful to me for coming to see him; he even left the Board Room after I had seen him and followed me down the passage to say that what I had done was absolutely right. Shortly after that Lord Harding arranged for the Board's staff to be brought together when, amongst other things, he said, 'No one here need fear for his job'. I was extremely pleased; I had done the right thing; a problem would be averted and I had received the congratulations of the Chairman. After such assurances we could all relax.

In October 1965 Brigadier H.J. de W. Waller was appointed Secretary of the Board. Brigadier Waller, usually called Sam, was head-hunted and resigned from the army especially to take the Levy Board position. Sam was a perfectly reasonable human being but it was not long before he was out of his depth. Like many army officers he knew a good deal about a number of things but he was not really proficient in any. He was one of those people who had been everywhere and was immensely confident that he could find the answer to any problem. He certainly would have known all about Rupert Brazier-Creagh and Paddy Victory, since he too had been a regular officer in the Royal Artillery. Sam had to pick up the reins which had been abandoned by Rupert. He had to continue the progress which was being made by the Levy Board in helping to finance all the avenues of racing where it was so desperately needed, and he had to face a staff problem of some complexity which should never have arisen. The two Assistant Secretaries, Victory and Catchpole, were incompatible and quarrelled over their responsibilities to such an extent that separate files for each racecourse had to be prepared for their respective purposes. We all wondered what the solution would be.

On 13 January 1966 Sam called me into his office to say that my position was being made redundant and I was being given three months notice ending on 30 April. I was truly knocked sideways. How Lord Harding came to agree with this proposal remains a mystery. Sam Waller had been very embarrassed at the interview and said that it had to be me who went because I was unmarried and had some private means. I immediately asked to see Lord Harding when I reminded him of his assurance that 'No one here need fear for his job'. He replied that he was sorry but he had to take the Secretary's advice.

The next day I received an official letter from the Secretary confirming my dismissal interview. In this letter the Secretary said, 'You are already aware that I will do all I can to assist you in obtaining another appointment in racing should you wish for one, and in the meantime the Board will go into the question of a redundancy payment. In conclusion, I would like to take this opportunity to thank you for the very good work you have done since you joined the Board staff in 1963.'

I have always assumed that the reason for so abrupt a

dismissal stemmed from Lord Harding's and Sam Waller's belief that they could easily find me another job in racing whereas this would have been almost impossible for any of the others. What right had Sam to refer to my private life when considering a staff problem created by the Board, and why did he think that I might be content to move sideways to some other job even if he could find one? They were surprised by the indication that I would fight and fight extremely hard, and so the notice of dismissal was withdrawn ten days later. The problem of too many executives, and of the wrong type, had not been solved and these events had a profoundly unsettling effect on a small organization. I had kept my job but I had not made myself very popular with people who had considerable influence over my future. I retained responsibility for veterinary affairs and all the other fringe activities which I valued so much and I hoped that time would heal some unpleasantly inflicted wounds.

CHAPTER 9

The Horserace Betting Levy Board – The Wigg Years
November 1967 to November 1972

IF 1965 AND 1966 were years of trauma and anxiety, 1967 was to be a year of peace and happiness. My position with the Board seemed to have been re-established when I received a letter from the Secretary, dated 17 November 1967, stating that 'it has been decided on grounds of merit and increased responsibility to raise your salary'. At 39 I was still single and early in the year my mother said to me that I ought to be married before I was 40. I achieved this on 24 October 1967, when I married Grania, daughter of Tom and Sighle Bevan from Castlebellingham. Grania's parents had been drowned in a boating accident in 1964, and we met through a mutual friend, Barbara Buxton, who brought her to a dinner party at 117 Dovehouse Street when someone dropped out at short notice. When we were engaged Grania told me that she was no good at anything except arranging flowers. This was an example of her modesty and it was not long before I realized how fortunate I was and that I was blessed with someone with all the qualities of a traditional wife. In view of the situation at the Levy Board I did, however, explain to Grania the difficulties which had arisen as I was well aware that they had not gone away, and the various personality clashes were such that they were bound to arise once again in due course. We were married at St

Mary's, Cadogan Street, Chelsea and our reception was at the Hyde Park Hotel. Our honeymoon was at the Mamounia Hotel in Marrakesh and we continued to live at Dovehouse Street. My house had been open to all with a stream of visitors who took advantage of bed and breakfast on an on-going basis, but that had to change when the new chatelaine arrived and at least one couple were disappointed when they tried to 'book-in' during our honeymoon.

Life at the Levy Board was temporarily uneventful. Lord Harding retired as Chairman in 1967. A Labour Government had been elected in 1964 after fifteen years of Tory rule. This was the first opportunity for a Labour administration to appoint a Chairman of the Board. There was never any doubt who would fill the appointment. George Wigg had served in the regular army between 1919 and 1937 and had rejoined in 1940 and had risen to the rank of Colonel in the Royal Army Education Corps. He had won Dudley for Labour in 1945 and had been Parliamentary Private Secretary to Emanuel Shinwell when he was Minister of Fuel and Power and Secretary of State for War in Mr Attlee's Government. He had been Paymaster General in the Wilson Government since 1964. He was without question extremely knowledgeable about racing, having served on the previous Racecourse Betting Control Board from 1958 and on the Horserace Totalisator Board which was established at the same time as the Levy Board in 1961. He was a true friend of racing and was an enthusiastic owner and punter. He had played a large part in the creation of the Levy Board and had been a key spokesman on behalf of the Labour Party. Nevertheless, the racing establishment feared him. He was a socialist and was unlikely to hobnob with the old aristocracy who still controlled racing even if they did

Wedding Day, 24 October 1967.

not control its finances in the way they wished.

George Wigg had, more than any other individual, paved the way for Harold Wilson's election victory in 1964. Almost single-handed he had flushed out Mr Profumo, who had resigned as Secretary of State for War from the Macmillan Government in 1963 after lying to the House of Commons over his affair with the prostitute, Christine Keeler. This had rocked the nation and had become the catalyst for so many changes which were to follow. While George may have done much to assist Labour back to power, he was not entirely welcome as a Cabinet Minister and his sinecure position as Paymaster General is evidence that he had reached his political peak. Harold Wilson was also well served by Marcia Williams, later Lady Falkender, who had been his private and political secretary and there was no room for both at the apex of Government. Harold needed to find a reward for George and the Chairmanship of the Levy Board was tailor-made for him. George became Chairman in November 1967 and the scene in racing was to change dramatically.

George Wigg was to be the Board's Chairman for five years, of which the first three would be mainly productive and the last two would be steeped in controversy. My initial relationship with George was normal and friendly. He recognized that I knew my subject and he himself was meeting personalities and finding out what could and should be done. Lord Harding, in spite of his experience in many fields, and in spite of his standing, had been unable to impose a realistic levy on the bookmakers. At that time the bookmakers recommended a levy scheme, but the Home Office-appointed members (the Chairman and two others) could impose their own scheme if, in the Board's opinion, the proposals from the bookmakers were inadequate. The proposals from the bookmakers were, of course, nearly always inadequate and the scheme imposed by the Board never yielded enough money to make sufficient impact on an underfunded industry. Mr Jack Carter, the second Chairman of the Bookmakers' Committee, which recommended the levy schemes, managed to persuade Lord Harding that the majority of bets placed in licensed betting offices (from which the bulk of the levy was derived) were in threepenny and sixpenny bets (pre-decimal currency). I doubt if any of the original members of the Board apart from General Feilden ever set foot in a betting shop to discover for themselves what went on. I had held on to my various responsibilities and was also assisting with racecourse improvements, prize money and the compilation of the fixture list. Many people in racing were, and still are, unaware that it is virtually impossible for a racecourse to stage a fixture without the approval of the Levy Board. It is the Levy Board which pays for the essential services without which racing cannot take place, such as the photo-finish, the camera patrol and all the licensed officials and security services. These services do not bring the public into racing but without them the integrity of the sport would not be maintained. It is worth noting that all these services are paid for by the punters through their lost bets and when the profits of the bookmakers and all the other grants are added in, it gives some idea of just how much money is lost by gambling on horses.

Like many people in his position in Government George Wigg had had the services of a civil servant to help him. I had remembered being met by such a person when I had visited Number 10 Downing Street early in 1967 when I had delivered introductory papers on behalf of Lord Harding and when I had had my first meeting with someone who was to have such an effect on my personal life. It did not therefore cause undue surprise when Reg McKenna joined the staff to supervise the collection of the levy. The Board Minutes of 15 July 1968 said:

> The Board has confirmed that the Secretary in consultation with Mr Hambro and Sir Alexander Sim (Chairman of the Tote) had offered the post of Assistant Secretary to Mr R. McKenna, a Treasury Official. Mr McKenna had accepted and hoped to join in September. Lord Wigg pointed out that should any redundancy be necessary in future among the Executive staff, Mr McKenna would, under the terms of the Fulton Report, be able to return to the Treasury. Since there had been a reduction in staff once before, he felt that there

was an important advantage in recognising the fact. He also wished to assure those at present in the service of the Board that their positions would not be placed in jeopardy should redundancy occur in the future.

This minute indicates that the Chairman knew all about the difficulties created by Lord Harding and Rupert Brazier-Creagh and also that at that time he was feeling his way carefully over questions of the staff. He had secured the appointment of a close ally who had worked with him before, and he had achieved this appointment in consultation with his Board.

A complete reorganization of the executive structure was to follow. Wigg was an experienced politician and he always liked to be able to prove that his actions were backed up by others. He did not like Lord Harding's men, but needed an authority to make the changes without which he could not exercise control in the way he wished. He therefore retained the Economist Intelligence Unit to undertake a survey in order to evaluate the effectiveness of the administrative structure and the methods and procedures adopted by the Board in the discharge of its statutory obligations. Nobody questioned whether the cost of this exercise was justified, but it should not have escaped the notice of the other members of the Board that the staff of some thirty-five was less than a Major's command, and it should not have been beyond them to undertake such a survey themselves if it was really considered necessary. An internal examination would not have suited Wigg. He wanted an independent firm whom he would pay, and above all whom he would brief. The report of the unit was submitted to the Board in February, 1969, and recommended a reorganization of the senior staff to provide for a Secretary, three other executives and an accountant: much the same as already existed but with different job descriptions and much increased salaries. On salaries the report said, 'The Board's incremental system of salary has been discontinued and salary scales based on merit and responsibility have been introduced'.

Wigg had decided that he was not compatible with Sam Waller, who probably felt the same way. Waller was the first to go and was replaced as Secretary in April 1969, by Paddy Victory who had accompanied Wigg on visits to racecourses, and also to the USA, throughout 1968, and had earned the nickname 'Noddy' as he always nodded his head in agreement with everything his master said. Waller's departure was followed later in the year by that of Bernard Catchpole who had been an Assistant Secretary since inception and Tom Russell who had been the worthy if rather ponderous accountant. Neither appeared to be unduly distressed and Tom was found a job by Lord Harding at Plessey Ltd. of which he was Deputy Chairman. I had hoped to continue with my various responsibilities but I realized that Wigg would like to be rid of me too. I was the youngest of the team apart from Paul Massey, another total 'yes' man who had been responsible for collecting the levy, and who was now to receive promotion.

It was at this time that I was befriended by Lord Kilmany who represented the National Hunt Committee on the Board; he was better known as Sir William Anstruther-Gray and had been Deputy Speaker of the House of Commons. He too was an experienced politician who was well aware of the ways of George Wigg, having been an adversary in Parliament for many years. He was a true friend of racing and was shrewd enough to recognize that my position was vulnerable for unpalatable reasons. He was concerned at the upheavals and did not want the Board to be staffed by placemen. He invited me to meet him at Brooks's (his London club) on 3 March 1969, to 'quiz' me and to suggest that I write to him in the event of difficulty. He had already intervened on my behalf at the Board Meeting on 28 February when the reorganization had been discussed. Little did I know then what a wonderful ally Bill Kilmany was to be or how soon I would need him. Wigg called me into his office on 6 March to ask me why I had not approached him to apply for one of the two jobs which remained in the light of the EIU Report. I told him that I thought it was for him to make the first move but that I very much wished to continue working for the Board. He then said that I was unsuitable for either and that I could not write English. Thus began his campaign to make me resign which was to continue for the remainder of his Chairmanship and which was to be carried on by others after his departure. He had managed to force Waller, Catchpole and Russell to resign and he thought he could do the same with me. Whereas the remaining executives were to receive substantial increases in salary in accordance with the recommendations, my salary was to be frozen on the basis that I was not worth any more. The final insult was that, despite having worked for the Board for six years, I was placed on six months' probation. The object was to force my resignation. I duly wrote at length to Lord Kilmany to thank him for his intervention and to acquaint him with what had transpired.

It was at this time that Gordon Hadden was appointed to oversee the Board's responsibilities to racecourses. He was a friend of McKenna's and had worked for the Treasury. There was no advertisement for the job and he was only interviewed by Wigg. In the summer of 1970 Wigg appointed Margaret Meades, another civil servant, who did not know the difference between odds against and odds on, as a back-up to Paddy Victory. Wigg had got to know Margaret during the dramatic negotiations with the Home Office on the rescue of the Tote which for three years had been unable to meet its obligations to the Board, and this culminated in her joining the staff of the Board; a job for a girl if ever there was one! This completed the team, none of whom apart from myself had the slightest knowledge of or interest in racing. Many times during the course of the next few years I had to listen to diatribes against the sport which gave them their living and which they said was lucky to have a levy at all. So long as Wigg was there he could and did control these people who had so little understanding of how racing worked, but he would not be there for ever. My position was made worse since they all knew that the Chairman did not want me, and they were jealous of the fact that my experience gave me the advantage of knowing virtually everyone with whom we were involved. Colleagues can be lethal and Wigg's appointees were to do all they could to help him with my removal. It was not that Wigg did not want me in racing, but that he did not want me at the Levy Board which could, if it wished, control the sport absolutely. Because of its financial muscle the Board was the final arbiter on every fixture, and this was to be even more apparent in years to come as arguments grew over the size of the fixture list. The degree of ignorance among my colleagues can be gauged from the fact that one of them, after working for the Board for no less than six years, confessed to me that he thought that the Jockey Club members of the Levy Board were the same people as the Stewards of the Jockey Club. It was truly frightening that these people had so much responsibility within the organization that controlled the whole destiny of racing. It was during 1969 that the friction between the Jockey Club and the Levy Board came out into the open when the Duke of Norfolk addressed the crowd at an autumn fixture at Ascot. Wigg was incensed that he should be criticized in public over a public address system which was paid for by his Board and he replied shortly afterwards in a speech at the Bollinger Dinner when he compared the Jockey Club to a well-kept veteran car. The seeds of disunity were truly sown.

Wigg had, however, achieved some notable successes. Since his appointment both the levy and the contribution to prize money had been doubled. From 1968 the levy was based on total turnover as opposed to the number of licensed betting offices. A differential was secured between the betting tax on-course and betting tax off-course, thus attracting spectators back to the racecourse. On-course tax would be eliminated in 1987 and general betting duty would be changed from a turnover to a gross profits tax as from October 2001. Perhaps his most significant success was the acquisition of Epsom, Sandown Park and Kempton Park and the creation of United Racecourses. Sandown Park in particular had been in danger of commercial exploitation and Wigg was probably the only person with sufficient drive and political expertise to negotiate with the various authorities to bring about the preservation of these three important racecourses for the benefit of racing. Kempton Park was sold to the Levy Board in 1970 by David Robinson, who had had his plans rejected by the Council, for some three quarters of a million pounds which was the same as he had paid for it the previous year.

Wigg's appointment in November 1967 had been for

three years. The Conservatives won the General Election in June 1970 and the time had arrived for his reappointment. Some people in high places would have liked to see him replaced, but this was unrealistic. Although he had made enemies, he had achieved a great deal in three years and had frightened the Jockey Club into listening to the industry as opposed to merely controlling it. I would have much liked to see him go and I had promised my wife, who was suffering as much as I was, that in the event of his reappointment I would leave. The Home Secretary, Reginald Maudling, confirmed the reappointment in July 1970 for a further two years expiring in November 1972. I duly informed my wife of this unpalatable news and she said, 'Right, you go'. I replied immediately, 'No, I stay'. In spite of the inevitable unpleasantness of a further two years I was convinced that I had to stay. Why should I leave a job which I enjoyed so much for political reasons, and what else was I qualified to do? Grania reluctantly accepted my decision and in years to come (and it was to be several more years before the injustices were put right) she would say that this was entirely correct.

If the first three years of Wigg's chairmanship of the Levy Board were beneficial to racing as a whole, the last two years were to result in friction with almost every section and every key person in the industry. Shortly after the reappointment I sat next to Lord and Lady Harding at a Farriers' Company dinner. Lord Harding was friendly and said that he had been made aware of my circumstances and he was also fully aware of all the unhappiness which had been created at every level. I did point out to Lord Harding that however difficult life was for the principals, they did not, as did the employees, have to live with a volatile situation every single day. A person with similar difficulties to myself was Peter Burrell, the long-serving Director of the National Stud who was responsible for the sale of the Gillingham and West Grinstead properties and the Stud's relocation to Newmarket in 1967, and who eventually retired in 1971. I worked closely with Peter, as I was Secretary of the Board's National Stud Committee from the time it was transferred from the Ministry of Agriculture in 1963 until 1969 when Wigg appointed Paul Massey in my place since he considered I was too friendly with the Director.

I realized that I would have to endure at least a further two years of purgatory but I was comforted by the fact that I had many friends out of the office. The standing of the Board had plummeted as a result of the Chairman's incessant rows with almost every authority, and in particular the Jockey Club and the Racecourse Association. The one way in which I could have been forced out would have been if I had been deprived of my responsibilities. However, apart from being removed from any association with the National Stud, my duties were increased. Because of the lack of expertise on the staff I was the only person capable of liaising in detail with the Jockey Club on prize money and fixture matters, and this I did on an almost daily basis with the expert Ken Allday who had been appointed 'Controller of Programmes', The absurdity of our relationship with Portman Square, where the Jockey Club offices were based, can be appreciated when a directive was given by Paddy Victory to all Levy Board staff that, 'All telephone calls to the Jockey Club are to be recorded and minuted and passed to the Secretary'. Suspicion was everywhere and this was to continue for a long time. My salary was almost permanently frozen, and I never participated in the substantial pay increases which were made to the other executives arising from recommendations in the EIU Report and to allow for the acceptance of Miss Meades. On one occasion, in July 1971, a full list of the staff was placed before the Board listing revised salaries which were duly approved. Even though I had then been with the Board for over eight years my name was deliberately omitted from the list, and in this way no revised salary was approved for me. I did find it extraordinary that no member of the Board thought fit to ask why my name was not on the list. I worked with all the Board members from time to time, and the two Home Office appointees had been members since the Board was established. The fact was that nearly everyone was frightened of Wigg. When he had first been appointed there was a Labour Government which was not considered friendly to racing or the Jockey Club, and the more he got away with it the more outrageous he became. He had found a simple way to freeze my salary.

He was determined to force me out and his unpleasantness was matched by the poison from Paddy Victory and Margaret Meades. In August 1971 Wigg called me to his office to say that he was looking for a suitable replacement for Malcolm Hancock as Clerk of the Course at Doncaster and Worcester, and a few days later he said he would assist me to become Clerk of the Course at York in place of Major Petch who was retiring. It was his view that these jobs would suit me well, but he overlooked the fact that neither job was within his giving and that I much preferred my administrative responsibilities with the Board. On another occasion he actually asked me why I did not resign, to which I replied immediately that I saw no reason to do so.

The acrimony between the Board and the industry

became public knowledge. I was approached by Timothy Kitson MP, whom I had known when my regiment was stationed at Catterick, and who was Parliamentary Private Secretary to Edward Heath, the Prime Minister, and he invited me to meet him to acquaint him with what was going on. Tim was both interested in and knowledgeable about all aspects of racing. We had met again at the Racehorse of the Year dinner on 5 June 1972 and I spent two hours with him at Number 10 Downing Street the next day. When I arrived for my appointment on the dot of 1 p.m. he remarked that I was very punctual, to which I replied that this was a meeting which I thought might be significant.

During this meeting I did not once refer to my own difficulties but concentrated on the need to find a new Chairman when Wigg's second term expired in November. Tim already knew much of what had been going on and said that the Government did not have anyone in mind at the moment but that it might be Sir Henry d'Avigdor Goldsmid who was to be made a member of the Horserace Totalisator Board in March 1973. His final words to me were that he would report on what I had told him to Mark Carlisle who was at that time Minister of State at the Home Office. There was little doubt that Wigg's time was coming to an end.

Shortly after this I went on holiday to Cyprus and returned to find that Paddy Victory had been sacked on 7 July 1972. He had left and would not appear again. Apparently he had been found drunk in the office and had been dismissed by Wigg for the same offence which brought about his departure from the army. While I was delighted to see the back of someone who had done all he could to undermine my position with the Board, I realized that his replacement by Margaret Meades would do nothing to ease my difficulties. Both of them were intensely jealous of the fact that I had so many contacts and that I had been with the Board since its earliest days. Wigg had no doubt seen Paddy for what he really was and was delighted to have the chance to replace him with his friend. Margaret's knowledge of racing had not advanced very far but her ability to do damage was limited while Wigg himself remained as Chairman.

The time for Wigg's final departure was fast approaching and I was determined that my own circumstances should be brought to light before he left. Each time he had discriminated against me I had asked for an explanation, and the answer was always the same, that my position was not allied to the Civil Service and that I was only 'attached to the staff'. I had very good friends in Lord Kilmany, General Sir Randle Feilden, Chairman of the Turf Board, and Sir John Ritchie, Chairman of the Board's Veterinary Advisory Committee, but none of them were in a position to do much other than offer encouragement. I knew that the Jockey Club members of the Levy Board were fully aware of the position and wanted to assist but, although immaterial, it did not help that two of three (the other two were Lord Crathorne and Lord Manton) were old Etonians and it would not have looked good if only they came to my rescue. I did notice Lord Kilmany, at one Board meeting when things were particularly difficult for me, wearing an old Etonian tie which I interpreted as an encouragement to me. That gesture was just possible then but would not be so today. Lord Kilmany was my self-appointed champion and it was to him I turned with steady correspondence. There were two problems: first, the affairs of the Board as a whole and its relationship with other organizations in the industry and second, my personal position.

At a distance of time it is difficult to realize just how ineffective the individual Board members were. The irregularities and the chicanery were discussed almost daily within racing's corridors of power but absolutely nothing was done. Nobody had any confidence that any confrontation with Wigg would be successful. A new Chairman would shortly be appointed and I decided to place my case history before the Deputy Chairman, Sir Denys Hicks. Hicks had been President of the Law Society in 1960 and on paper was an ideal choice to be a Home Office appointee when the Board was established in 1961. Sadly he was one of the most ineffective individuals I have ever met and was to make no real contribution in his sixteen years of service other than always to agree with the Chairman. The chance of his standing up to Wigg on any issue was non-existent. He was both in appearance and in committee a real mouse of a man. He was, however, Deputy Chairman, and he could not be other than aware of the unhappiness within both the Levy Board itself and also within the industry. He did attend all Board Meetings and many Committee Meetings but his lack of initiative was matched only by his silence.

The other Home office appointee was Mr Grant Munro, an accountant from Scotland who served from inception until he died in February 1977. He too on paper was an ideal choice with his expertise in financial matters and as a representative of Scotland. Like Hicks he was totally ignorant of racing and came under the spell of George Wigg to such an extent that he opposed almost every request from the various racing associations. With the two Home Office appointees in his pocket Wigg had been able to do as he wished.

It was, therefore, to Sir Denys Hicks that I submitted my

case history and I duly wrote to him on 12 July 1972. I wrote from home as follows:

> Dear Sir Denys,
>
> I forward the enclosed 'case history' to you for your information.
>
> It had been my intention to hand it to the new Chairman of the Levy Board as and when he took office, but in view of recent events I have thought it more correct to pass it to you now in your capacity as Deputy Chairman of the Levy Board since inception.
>
> The object of passing this case history to you at this juncture is not to ask you to take any action but is merely to let you know about circumstances of which, in my opinion, you ought to be informed. With your length of service you will also be in a position to follow the train of events.
>
> As I have already said it had been my intention to hand this story, at an appropriate moment, to the next Chairman of the Levy Board. To have adopted this course would have been easy, but I feel I would be failing the Board as a whole if I were to take this easy way out.
>
> You will appreciate that many statements of fact in this case history are backed up by either letters which are in my possession or by the actual Minutes of the Board.
>
> I would be failing in my duty as a servant of the Board, and this is the important part of this letter, if I did not say that the time for intervention and examination of what goes on in this office is now long overdue. It is overdue not by weeks or by months but by years. This opinion is shared in different degrees by my colleagues.
>
> The crux of so many problems is that on issue after issue and subject after subject the Board is provided with only part of the story. Decisions are then either rescinded or are questionable with serious results on our relationships both with each other and with outside organizations.

I have thought long and hard as to whether or not to write to you, but in the belief that you must surely want to know the truth I have passed to you this letter, and I am also sending a copy of both the letter and the case history to Lord Kilmany since I think that a Jockey Club member of the Board should be informed.

Yours sincerely

M.R.C. Crawshay

This letter was accompanied by my case history which listed in ten pages the events from Paddy Victory's arrival to my dismissal under Lord Harding and the catalogue of what amounted to cheating and discrimination on a massive scale under Lord Wigg. A copy of the case history is included as an Appendix. I wondered what would happen. The letter had been copied to Lord Kilmany, and surely such damning evidence could not be overlooked. I waited. I never received any reply and Hicks never said a word to me about it during the remaining four years that he was Deputy Chairman of the Board. Lord Kilmany told me that he had spoken to him about it but did not say what he had said. Nevertheless, I was relieved that I had submitted a case history to the right person at the right time.

Wigg duly retired in 1972 only to become President of the Betting Office Licensees' Association: a real example of gamekeeper turned poacher. He had seen the levy increase steadily during his Chairmanship of the Board, and so long as he was Chairman he was happy about that but he did not want anyone else to have the opportunity of spending what he saw as the income he had raised. At the time of his departure he was seriously concerned that the income from the levy would increase too much, and so his departure to the camp of the bookmakers gave him the opportunity to continue to be involved with racing politics and to provide the opposition which he thought would be necessary.

For myself I was thankful to see the back of him and I said to friends that the appropriate inscription on my tombstone would be, 'This man survived Lord Wigg'.

However, any expectation that my life would be any easier under Sir Stanley Raymond, who was appointed to succeed Lord Wigg, would soon be disappointed.

CHAPTER 10

The Horserace Betting Levy Board – Discrimination Continues
1972-1973

THE HOME SECRETARY who appointed Sir Stanley Raymond to be Chairman of the Board was Robert Carr, created Lord Carr of Hadley in 1975. The Levy Board was never much of a priority in the affairs of the Home Office and no one can say who recommended this appointment. Sir Stanley had been Chairman of the Gaming Board since its inception in 1968, and the understanding was that the Government considered it a good idea to bring the two organizations associated with gambling under the same umbrella. Lord Harding's original appointment had been part-time to suit his circumstances and the original set-up with a Secretary well versed in the affairs of racing could not have been questioned. The appointment had been made full-time to suit Lord Wigg and this again could not be questioned in view of his commitment. Sir Stanley's was once again a part-time appointment, which suited his circumstances, but one wonders whether the authorities ever really considered what racing required and whether or not the Chairman of the Levy Board should have been a full-time appointment from the outset. One Home Secretary who did try to help the Levy Board was Roy Jenkins who contacted Jakie Astor (George Wigg's pair when both were members of the House of Commons, and later an influential member of the Board) to ask him to suggest a Home Office nominee, and the recommendation was John Marriage who joined the Board in 1976.

Sir Stanley Raymond had been brought up in an orphanage and had risen to Lieutenant-Colonel in the Royal Artillery during his service in the Second World War. He had previously been a civil servant and his post-war experience was in transport, culminating with the Chairmanship of British Railways between 1965 and 1967. He had no particular knowledge of horseracing but was an experienced administrator and no doubt he was told that his lack of knowledge of racing might even be an advantage because the Board had been established for eleven years and was administered by an experienced staff. He would have been surprised to find what he did.

Lord Wigg, who will probably be rightly credited for achieving more in his five years of office than any other Chairman, did not make any preparations for his successor. The senior staff which he left behind were, with the exception of myself, chosen by him to suit his purposes. Any responsible Commanding Officer will always recognize that he will in due course hand over his responsibilities to some other person and will act accordingly, but a valid criticism of Wigg is that he never considered his successor for one moment. The industry had become totally dependent on the Levy Board, and everyone was looking forward to working with the new Chairman in more harmonious circumstances than during the recent past. A disadvantage of any change at the top is that the rate of progress inevitably slows down but this has to be accepted. In September 1972, only two months before his departure, Lord Wigg had made one final appointment to the staff of the Board. He had approached the Treasury and arranged for the release of Donald Stewart, then 35, in order that he might act as back-up to Margaret Meades in the same way as she had acted as support for Paddy Victory before his dismissal. Donald was later to become a respected secretary of the National Stud Committee and to become responsible for the Board's support for racecourse buildings, but at the time of joining the whole subject of betting and racing was new to him. The expertise available to Sir Stanley Raymond was therefore somewhat deficient. It may seem surprising that the circumstances which have been described did not give rise to any co-ordinated complaint from the industry, but the money from the Board was always distributed and our internal difficulties were of little concern to the beneficiaries so long as financial support continued to flow.

I hoped that with a new Chairman the injustice whereby I received a much lower salary than all the other executives in spite of having served longer than any of them would be corrected. I retained all my responsibilities for veterinary affairs, grants to the horse societies, prize money and fixture business, apprentice training, and grants to point-to-points and farriery. This was a substantial portfolio with wide contacts and reflected a substantial part of the Board's expenditure. There had been what was known as a Staff Establishment Committee until it was virtually ignored by Wigg, but they had never been properly briefed and so had become ineffective. All staff matters were therefore handled by the Chairman who might, or might not, report accurately to the Board.

On 16 November 1972 Lord Kilmany told me that the Chairman would speak to me about my salary and suggested that I should wait until he brought the matter up. I recognized that this was obviously correct and accepted his advice. Lord Kilmany spoke to me again on 15 January 1973 when he again said that the Chairman would speak to me on the subject of my salary and, of course, I was extremely pleased and grateful to him for taking this initiative. However, nothing happened.

I had close contact with the new Chairman and together we attended the Stallion Shows of the Hunters' Improvement Society on 8 March and the Shire Horse Society on 28 March. Sir Stanley was to show particular interest in the horse societies and found the 'atmosphere' more to his taste than the sectional interests of the racing industry as a whole. The grants to the horse and pony societies were all considerably increased over the years, and the annual grant to the Shire Horse Society, which was primarily applied to stallion premiums, increased from £500 at the inception of the Board to £38,000 by the time I retired in 1991. The assistance from the Board, which was minuscule in the context of the racing budget, was to be the salvation of some of the breeds which suffered from the fact that the horse was no longer considered to be an agricultural animal in the eyes of the Government. The Shire Horse Society owed its success to the versatile Roy Bird whose leadership and determination over many years was to convince characters as diverse as Bill Whitbread (late Chairman of Whitbread's Brewery), George Wigg and Stanley Raymond, that this was a society which had to be supported. My responsibilities were to make sure that the case was properly presented and, while I could not guarantee success, a false move would have wrecked the application.

My day with Sir Stanley on 28 March at the Shire Horse Society Stallion Show at Peterborough gave me the opportunity to talk to him on a number of subjects. Colonel Whitbread, who was President of the Society, provided a car to take us from London to Peterborough and back. The day was successful and I duly wrote to Lord Kilmany the following day. This letter is reproduced below as it indicates what I was able to say to Sir Stanley on this my first opportunity for a private discussion since his appointment the previous November.

Dear Lord Kilmany,

You will remember that you mentioned to me last November and last January that the Chairman would be speaking to me on the subject of my pay. You suggested, and I agreed, that it would be better for me to await an approach from him. As you well know, I was grateful to you for what you said and I concluded that you had probably spoken to the Chairman and told him the unhappy story.

It has been disappointing in view of all the circumstances that the Chairman has not in fact spoken to me about this, but yesterday I did accompany him alone to Peterborough and back for the Shire Horse Society Stallion Show. Colonel Whitbread kindly sent a car for us and so the opportunity was there for the Chairman to say anything he felt necessary.

I would like to say at the outset that the Chairman could not have been more friendly and the journey was considerably easier than I had anticipated. Nearly all the way up he asked me numerous questions on a variety of subjects with which I am concerned and particularly apprentice training, grants to Horse Societies and Prize Money. I was able to answer virtually everything he asked easily enough – except why the Board stopped the grant to the Olympic Games – I attributed this to the peculiarities of our late Chairman. He told me that in his conversations with members of the Board they had agreed with him that not enough was spent on the improvement of the breeds. We discussed this at length, particularly as it affected our business of the day which will eventually come back to you, and in view of his interest I did say that the increased grant to the Shire Horse Society was in fact achieved only on the casting vote of Lord Wigg and after numerous references back to the Board.

The journey back was equally friendly but was the opportunity for some of the more difficult matters. He told me that he was completely at one with General Feilden, and I followed this up by saying that would be an immense relief to everyone in racing. I referred to the harm that had been done in the past by the differences between the Jockey Club and Levy Board and that all this controversy was unnecessary. From this we moved on to our own office, and it came as a shock to me to discover how little he knew about what has gone on. He had hardly heard of Rupert Brazier-Creagh, knew practically nothing of the E.I.U. Report, and nothing at all of Sam Waller's arrival or departure. He was completely ignorant of Victory's arrival and what followed from that, but did say 'wasn't he an alcoholic?'.

I found my task made much more difficult by the fact that he seemed wholly unaware of the dreadful things that have gone on. Why I wonder has no one informed him?

I told him that for ages it had been a very unhappy office, and that as a result of the constant changes confidence had been lost by everyone and that this affected the ability of people to make any kind of stand when this was required. I made no mention whatever of my pay but to illustrate the appalling degree of incompetence I did mention in detail the circumstances of Rupert's departure, Victory's arrival, and my dismissal under Lord Harding. I said I felt I could not make any comment on anyone still with us but that no harm could come of stating the facts of the fairly distant past. I explained to him that Victory was suffering from the same complaint when he arrived as he was when he left, that there was no job for him when he arrived and that eventually I was supposed to be pushed out to make room. I pointed out that he had been given a job even though he had just been dismissed from the Army while in command of his Regiment, and this after interview by the Field Marshal, Sir Denys Hicks and Sir Alexander Sim! I told the Chairman that this was an episode which people just would not believe possible. Nevertheless it is true.

Apart from a passing reference to having once stayed with you I made no comment whatsoever about my correspondence with you, or my discussions with you, with the General or anyone else. I made no mention of anyone's name now on the staff. I did say that the internal dealings of the Levy Board had been utterly dreadful and I did say that he was bound to find out the truth in the end even if it took him five years. He asked me bits and pieces about Brazier-Creagh, Sam Waller and Victory, and as I say, the questions indicated that he had virtually no knowledge of what has gone on.

If he had known more I could have said more, and I think he wanted to know. He was obviously interested but I doubt if he realized how these events have damaged the whole structure and image of the Board.

I feel that it was a useful day from the Chairman's point of view, and I am sure I could not have gone further.

I have written to you at length because you are the one person who has shown a proper interest in our affairs throughout, and in view of what you have done for me in the past I owe it to you to keep you informed as to matters of fact.

As I have always respected your confidence I know you will respect mine as far as the Chairman is concerned. However may I now ask what is going to be done about my pay? You said the Chairman would speak to me about it and he has not yet done so. This business has cost me and my family dreadful unhappiness apart from literally thousands!

May I ask you the direct question as to whether injustice is to be put right or whether I have wasted ten years of my life? I feel sure that if the Chairman really knew what has gone on and where the blame lay that things would be different.

May I end by saying again that I am grateful for your support but the the problem is one which the Board will have to face sometime.

Yours, etc.

Lord Kilmany replied on 1 April 1973:

Dear Martin

Thank you for your letter of 29th March. I am so glad you have had an opportunity of a personal talk to our Chairman.

If you want me to talk to the Chairman I will do so when he comes to Kilmany on 17th April. I remain of the opinion that his talk to you about your affairs should emanate from him – without prompting by me or anybody else, but I agree with you that you cannot wait for ever.

Yours, sincerely, Kilmany

This was somewhat disappointing since he had twice indicated to me that he had already prompted the Chairman, but my own letter clearly indicated that the full story had not been divulged. I had come to realize that the whole subject had become incredibly delicate and was too hot to handle. Nevertheless, my letter of 12 July 1972 to Sir Denys Hicks and now this letter of 29 March 1973 could hardly be accepted unchallenged and ignored.

I was encouraged to receive a second letter from Lord Kilmany a few days later, as follows:

DISCRIMINATION CONTINUES

11th April 1973

Dear Martin

Well done with the Vets. I thought it went well and, in particular, thank you for looking after me.

We did not, as things turned out, have an opportunity to talk to each other – nor will we have an opportunity on Monday.

I would still prefer the initiative to come from the Chairman. I will, however, do the best I can to put the idea into his head – but all very gently, because I don't know him at all well yet.

Let me repeat that I myself am on your side.

Yours, K

The reference to the Vets by Lord Kilmany is a reference to the first Veterinary Conference which was organized by the Board to present the results of work sponsored by the Board to a lay audience from the industry. Attendance was from many branches of the equine world, and this particular gathering took place at the Field Station of the Royal Veterinary College and also marked the retirement of Sir John Ritchie after twelve years as Chairman of the Board's Veterinary Advisory Committee. The Conference was sufficiently successful that similar Conferences were organized every five years and mostly took place at the Royal Society.

Sir Stanley naturally attended the Veterinary Conference which, in this instance, lasted two days, and I hoped that since the organization was entirely my responsibility it would reflect creditably on my administrative ability. Now that he had been in office for six months I hoped he would do something to rectify the injustice surrounding my salary and my position *vis-à-vis* my colleagues. At the following

Board Meeting on 21 May I was once again given private encouragement by Lord Kilmany who said to me privately that he would resent the situation enormously if he were in my position, but we had both agreed that the first move must come from the Chairman himself. Lord Kilmany suggested that I should 'engineer' a means of talking to him.

Later the same day Margaret Meades told me that the Chairman was aware of my salary position and wanted to know why I had been running to Board members. I replied that I had not been running to Board members but that I had answered Lord Kilmany's questions. Four days later on 25 May I decided to act and I handed in the following letter to Sir Stanley:

> Dear Chairman
>
> I understand from Margaret Meades that you are aware of the situation regarding my salary.
>
> It may be, however, that the circumstances whereby my salary has been separated from the basis adopted for the other Executives have not been revealed.
>
> I would be grateful indeed if you will let me know whether or not this situation will be rectified.
>
> Yours sincerely, etc.

Nothing further occurred until Sir Stanley called me in to his office on 20 July when he bluntly told me that I was adequately paid for the work I did and made no reference to discrimination. I duly handed him a copy of the case history which I had submitted to Sir Denys Hicks in the previous July, and he did at least say that that had been correct procedure. Nothing further was gained, but I had meetings with him on three further occasions before I wrote on 19 October to Lord Kilmany as follows:

DISCRIMINATION CONTINUES

Dear Lord Kilmany

I expect you will know that the Chairman has been making enquiries into the circumstances of my position with the Board, and since I know that these circumstances have been of concern to you I think you may be interested to hear from me what has gone on and how it has ended.

I refrained from mentioning the subject until Miss Meades said on 21st May that the Chairman was aware of my salary position. Then, in view of the nature of the story, and knowing that the Chairman must have been told a good deal by this point of time, I placed a letter on his desk, a copy of which I attach.

Nothing happened until 20th July when the Chairman called me to his office and acknowledged receipt of the letter. He also said he had examined my file and that it was his opinion that my salary adequately reflected the work I did for the Board. Since he seemed to have already decided the issue I mentioned that he had not asked me anything about the case, and told him I had submitted a copy of the history to Sir Denys Hicks and to you last July. I told him that I had done this so that the case could be brought to light while his predecessor was in office, and, at his request, gave him a copy which was identical in every respect to what you have seen.

Since 20th July I have seen the Chairman some three times on this subject, and I do not intend to weary you with a verbatim report, but suffice it to say that he has decided to maintain the status quo. He has told me that he has talked to lots of people and none of them has said that I am underpaid. He says my file reveals that it has all been explained to me. In my interviews I have said that I would not expect anyone to say that I was underpaid, and that my complaint (He said, 'What is your complaint?') is discrimination. I am afraid the Chairman has never referred to this aspect nor to the fact that I do exactly the same work as anyone else.

The upshot of all this is that the Chairman has refused to treat me equally with the others, but has offered to give me a salary rise in my present grade at the turn of the year. At the same time he has instructed me not to refer to the matter again.

Several times the Chairman has indicated that he is well aware of the truth. He has said amongst other things that he does not intend to have an enquiry, that he does not wish to have a 'Crichel Down' situation, and that the case history I presented is the truth as I see it. Nevertheless he has again and again come back to the point that I am not underpaid for the work I do and that according to my file Lord Wigg was of the opinion that I was 'not up to it'.

This is really very serious as I have waited and waited for something to be done, and over the years I have handled a very large part of the Board's affairs. There is no doubt in my mind that Lord Wigg is determined I should not succeed at the Board, and that he has again been consulted and has ensured that the policy will continue. It is clear to me that the Chairman has taken no account of anything you or anyone favourable to me may have said, or to the facts in my case history. He has taken no account of what Sir John Ritchie may have written to him or of what he can see are my responsibilities for the Board. He has instead listened to the same people who have brought this situation to pass and who are now benefiting from it. He read to me an extract from Sir Denys Hicks's letter, and I can only say that for a past President of the Law Society it was pitiful.

Since the Chairman is determined to go by my file I enclose a copy of an extract. This entry is libellous, and will prove to you, if proof you need, that there has been deliberate misrepresentation.

Unfortunately it is not easy to move from here and such attempts I have made have not been successful. I have now put up with so much that I cannot resign, but I recognise that the forces against me are very strong indeed even though no one would admit to being a party to what has been done.

I believe someone must have suggested that there ought to be an 'enquiry'. This would be the only hope of establishing the truth, but the Chairman is obviously determined that there should be no such thing. It is a travesty that while the Board is prepared to pose the most searching questions at everyone else their own organisation is open to grave criticism.

I would have liked to have walked out but I am not in a position to do so. I know that you will be sorry at the turn of events. It must be a fact that I could not have revealed the story to you, to Sir Denys and now to the Chairman and have remained in my job without anyone contradicting what I have said unless it were true. I am worried about what happens when you eventually retire as there will then be nobody who could assist in putting this right, but in the end the truth is bound to come out as it always does.

If the matter is ever to be put right the only place is across the Board Room table, and this can only be done if people say in public what they say in private and if they follow through to the bitter end. The damage done within the Board is considerable as both the Executives and members of the staff know the story depending on how long they have been here. There is a repercussion in that seeing the way things are done people are reluctant to stand up for principles anywhere and consequently no one ventures against the party line.

I sometimes wonder if the Board Members appreciate the difficulties. As a simple example I did much to rescue the Point-to-Point grants which will come before you shortly. They had almost been abandoned as being 'grants to rich hunts' until I had the opportunity of explaining what they were about and why they were paid. This particular problem is now back on the rails but nevertheless in certain quarters it has done me no good.

I must again thank you for all you have done and I am naturally very disappointed that such obvious injustice should continue.

All I ask for is fair play.

Yours sincerely, etc.

Lord Kilmany was obviously very disappointed by my letter. A few days later we met after a Board meeting when he indicated that further intervention by him, who had no particular responsibility for internal matters, was unlikely to yield any different result. Further patience was the only course of action.

The reference by the Chairman to a 'Crichel Down' situation was significant. Crichel Down had been a *cause célèbre* when the Minister of Agriculture, Sir Thomas Dugdale, later Lord Crathorne and a member of the Board, resigned from the Government in 1954 following an enquiry brought by a member of the public into the mishandling of property by his Department. It had caused an outcry at the time and the Minister accepted responsibility for gross incompetence by his officials and resigned. The fact that Sir Stanley mentioned this himself is a clear indication that he was fully aware of the implications and what might be the outcome of any enquiry. It was also clear that Sir Stanley had been influenced by a discussion he had had with Lord Wigg who had an obsession that I must not succeed at the Levy Board.

I was deeply disappointed and it was at this time that I responded to an advertisement by the Racehorse Owners' Association who were looking for a Secretary (later to be called a Director-General) for their organization. I was called for interview and was offered the job over lunch by the then President, Louis Freedman, and Frank Beale and Christopher Collins. I was immensely grateful to them for this offer but immediately declined to accept. Despite pressure I maintained my position which they reluctantly accepted. I apologized to them for any inconvenience I had caused and explained that I needed to find reassurance for myself which their offer had provided. They had an alternative candidate and so they were not unduly put out, and my confidence in myself duly increased. Little did my enemies know how close they had come to achieving their objective. There was no alternative but to soldier on and I still so much enjoyed my work. I had received further comfort from a tribute paid to me by Sir John Ritchie when he attended his last meeting with the Levy Board on 17 September when he was effusive in his praise for my assistance in veterinary affairs over the previous ten years.

Life is indeed extraordinary. Just when I had so little to look forward to, Sir Stanley Raymond resigned as Chairman of the Board as from 21 January 1974. This was completely unexpected and was partly due to his wife's illness and partly because he disliked the industry with which he was so closely associated. He ended his fifteen months' term of office by publicly rebuking those who had clamoured for an increase in the levy when he said: 'There are some engaged in horseracing who do not seem to appreciate the privileged position the sport is in when compared to other sports of equal or greater public appeal. A subsidy of now well over £7m a year is a considerable help. This is public money and the Levy Board have to ensure that it is spent for the good of horseracing as a whole and not for private gain.' Looking back Sir Stanley said it had been stimulating to complete and open the new Sandown, to negotiate for the retention of Mill Reef at the National Stud and to lay the foundations and establish the guidelines for the two major enquiries now underway into the future requirements of the sport and manpower associated with it. His unsolicited press statement came as a surprise. Its wording suggested he was far from happy with the administration of racing as he had observed it: that particularly, he found the constant lobbying for more public money unedifying and distasteful, and that he wanted everybody to know it. Perhaps significantly, his farewell message made no mention of pleasure derived from working with those with whom his job brought him into contact, as farewell messages often do. His references to public money were somewhat inaccurate as money raised by the levy could only be spent in application of purposes laid down in the 1963 Act, and no one before or since has ever indicated that it was spent for private gain.

For myself, I had no regrets. Sir Stanley had done nothing to correct what I saw was an obvious injustice, and I had long realized that he was not in sympathy with the industry which depended on him. I also recognized that he had no chance when he was served by a staff of whom most had so little understanding of why the Board had been established in the first place.

This was the Levy Board's lowest point but a new chapter was about to begin.

CHAPTER 11

The Horserace Betting Levy Board – Sir Desmond Plummer
1974-1982

THE NEW Chairman of the Board, from 22 January 1974, was Sir Desmond Plummer, later in 1981 to be appointed a life peer, who had previously been Leader of the Greater London Council. He was hardly known in racing circles but much hope was once again placed in someone with a track record in administration. In order to assist him with his new responsibilities the Board's executives were required to prepare 'Briefs' to help his understanding of how the Board's financial assistance was applied. My briefs covered prize money, the fixture list, farriery, grants to horse and pony societies, point-to-points, apprentice training and veterinary science and veterinary education: a fairly detailed and complex list. These headings were reviewed in detail annually and, with an increasing levy, benefited from whatever extra money was available.

Sir Desmond's first move was to bring in Tristram Ricketts, a fourth-generation Wykehamist, and grandson of Sir Stafford Cripps, the Chancellor of the Exchequer in Clement Attlee's post-war Labour Government, who had been his personal assistant at the Greater London Council. Tristram was then 27 and knew nothing about racing but, as had become the usual practice, was brought in with a salary much in excess of mine. At first Sir Desmond had been told that there was no room for an extra person, but the opportunity arrived when McKenna decided to retire and Don Stewart was made responsible for collecting the levy. Tristram became assistant to Margaret Meades, and in particular as special assistant to the new Chairman whose ways he already knew so well.

Tristram was perhaps the cleverest man I have met and was soon to become an expert on every aspect of racing administration. He absorbed knowledge with unusual speed and efficiency and came to know everything there is to know apart from blood-lines. He was to become the pillar on which three Chairmen of the Levy Board were to lean until he became Chief Executive of the British Horseracing Board in 1993. My relationship with him was friendly and I gave him all the help I could, just as I had done to all previous new arrivals. He quickly assessed the position in our small office and on 22 May 1974 he told me that he thought the place deserved to fall apart and could not understand why it did not. He obviously had confidence in me as he also asked me what I thought should be done about it. It hardly needed me to explain about mismanagement at the top, but I took the opportunity to show him a copy of my letter of 12 July 1972 to Sir Denys Hicks.

We all knew it was Tristram who had the ear of the Chairman rather than Margaret Meades and he became more and more responsible day by day.

I no longer felt threatened, and it was clear that it was now Margaret Meades herself who was sidelined. The Chairman looked to Tristram for advice on every matter, and it was clear that he really did not want anyone else. Tristram, being an excellent communicator, eased the tensions both in and out of the office and some harmony was gradually restored. I have always assumed it was due to him that the discrimination against me was eventually ended and that my salary was increased to the level of my colleagues. This actually happened on 20 January 1975 when Sir Desmond called me into his office to say that I was being regraded and that he hoped this would finish the unfortunate business for ever. The meeting with Sir Desmond was followed by an official letter from Margaret Meades redesignating my position and revising my salary.

I was, of course, delighted. The decision of Sir Desmond, almost a year after taking up his appointment, vindicated my campaign to correct the injustices which I had endured for some seven years. It meant that what I had written in my case history was accepted, and I knew that this must be so since no one had ever contradicted anything I had said. I immediately wrote to Lord Kilmany who had continued to support me throughout 1974 and who had recently retired from the Board, and I received the following reply from the House of Lords dated 27 January:

Dear Martin,
   Thank you very much for your letter. I had, in fact, heard your good news when sitting next to the Chairman at dinner last Monday.
   That it should have taken so long for you to establish your rights made me, as you know, quite indignant quite often but my indignation achieved nothing!
   Within a month of my departure, however, 'the penny drops', and all is well!
   I am so delighted for your sake.
   All good wishes, yours sincerely
   Kilmany

While many people had encouraged me privately, I had had to fight a very long and lonely battle against powerful and determined enemies and I certainly would not have survived without the support of Lord Kilmany and Sir John Ritchie, and also my loyal secretary Margaret Healy who typed many long letters and looked after every aspect of my work. To them I express my thanks and appreciation. While my immediate problems were over I was well aware that I would never be accepted by Margaret Meades. Margaret was a disciple of George Wigg and her every action was in pursuit of his endeavours. It was about this time that there was once again a sea-change in the office. Sir Desmond tried to arrange for Margaret to be returned to the Home Office but senior Home Office officials would have none of it. What actually was said is not known, but from then on until her retirement at the end of 1979 Margaret exercised her influence and this appeared to be accepted by Sir Desmond who, despite his earlier attempt to remove her, even recommended her for an honour which was duly awarded in the form of an OBE in 1978. His change of attitude can only be described as strange indeed and it stemmed from his encounter with Home Office officials. It was well known that Sir Desmond's ambition was to become a life peer and he was anxious that nothing should be done which could in any way be interpreted as being anti-Government. In the meantime Tristram Ricketts was appointed Deputy Secretary in 1976, confirming his position as number two in the organization.

A feature of the racing industry in the 1960s and 1970s was the number of studies and enquiries into some aspect of its well-being. They were almost continuous and virtually all pointed to underfunding and excessive taxation.

No enquiry was to be more important than the Royal Commission on Gambling which sat between 1976 and 1978 under the Chairmanship of Lord Rothschild. The Board submitted written evidence in 1976 and this was supplemented by the Chairman's oral evidence a year later, but for reasons which were never made clear the Board did not publish its evidence in full, although copies of it were, together with other written evidence to the Commission, placed in the House of Commons library and other libraries. That Margaret had undue influence on the Board's evidence was apparent. This was once again a time of considerable hostility between the Jockey Club and the Levy Board. Both organizations were concerned with power and it probably came as a shock to Sir Desmond that his proposals were totally rejected by the recommendations of the Royal Commission which proposed a new style British Horseracing Authority, with the Jockey Club being charged with producing an acceptable constitution for such an authority. The report of the Royal Commission revealed that the Board had shown interest in increasing its control over the fixture list, the number of racecourses and the contribution which racecourses made to prize money.

I was concerned at the secrecy surrounding the Board's evidence to the Royal Commission, and I was particularly alarmed about what had been submitted on Levy Board staffing, which was as follows:

> The Board is at present a comparatively small organization whose staffing levels are kept to a minimum in the interests of efficiency and economy. Opportunities for promotion are very limited and there is no career structure. There are inherent problems with this lack of mobility.

> To overcome this problem the Board would wish to be staffed like the Gaming Board, by established Civil Servants so that there can be free interchange of staff between Government Departments and the Board. This would be likely to be to the mutual advantage of all concerned.

I was certain that this was exactly what was not required. My experience of the civil servants with whom we had had contact in the Home Office was that they were not particularly friendly to racing and they were always unaware of the difficulties of an industry which at that time was taxed to breaking point. Part of the reason for their lack of understanding may well have been because of the deliberately inadequate briefing which came from the Levy Board itself. My experience of civil servants who had joined us, and with whom I had worked, was enough to alert me that any implementation of such a proposal would be disastrous for racing. There was no parallel with the Gaming Board whatsoever.

I therefore wrote on 8 October 1976 to John Macdonald-Buchanan, who was then the senior Jockey Club member of the Levy Board, to alert him to what I saw as a serious error and a determination that people like myself who had given years of service, and who had a knowledge of the industry, would not even be eligible for consideration for a place on the staff of any new authority. I pointed out to him that no one on the Board's staff, apart from Margaret Meades and Tristram Ricketts, had seen the paper which had been placed before the Board at its September meeting, and they had therefore had no opportunity to comment on any aspect of the submission.

John Macdonald-Buchanan duly replied four days later. His comments were revealing:

You are quite right in saying that most members of the Board, and particularly the Jockey Club ones, had very strong reservations about the part of the submission to the Royal Commission which proposed that the staffing should be by civil servants.

As you probably realize there were considerable areas of the submission where we were obliged to dissent. Therefore eventually we were persuaded to agree to this particular paragraph (relating to staffing). We were given a very full explanation by the Chairman of what his implications and intentions were, and as we considered it a domestic matter we therefore reluctantly agreed. Of course as you say the presentation to us may be a travesty of the truth and I quite accept what you have said in your letter.

We do in fact now know that none of the Executives except Miss Meades and Mr Ricketts had seen the paper but this has only come to our attention recently and we have been somewhat surprised about this, to say the least. Unfortunately, and as I think you must know, the submission has now been forwarded to the Royal Commission and therefore it is rather late for any action to be carried out at this stage. However, I think it is probably possible that the matter can be raised again sometime fairly soon, but it is of course unfortunate that it has now gone to the Commission apparently without dissent.

This confirmed my fears and was one more example of how the Jockey Club members of the Board appeared unable to exert adequate influence when it was imperative that they should do so.

I had come to distrust Sir Desmond Plummer who appeared to me to be more interested in advancing his own career than he was in the promotion of horseracing. Any lingering respect I had for him vanished when, after giving his oral evidence to the Commission, he spoke to the Executives on 6 September 1977 and told us that we should not over-react to the evidence on staffing and that we should have nothing to fear. He completely ignored the fact that we had not been consulted and the whole history of Levy Board staffing had revolved around placemen. It was little short of disgraceful that a Statutory Board which liked to present itself as whiter than white did not publicly advertise a single post between 1965 and 1985, during which time three Secretaries were sacked and other executives were forced to resign. Racing is highly technical and much specialist knowledge is required if an administrator is to be able to adjudicate on the endless problems which present themselves on an almost daily basis. My criticism of my employers was that they did not learn from their own mistakes and were highly critical of everyone else. In the end the Board's evidence to the Royal Commission did not matter and certainly Lord Rothschild was able to make sensible recommendations which would, in due course, pave the way for the kind of authority which racing so badly needed, and which had been recommended by the Benson Report some ten years earlier. The Levy Board would have done well to take heed of a statement by the Senior Steward, Lord Howard de Walden, who emphasized as a central issue that 'the administrative structure of the sport must be largely in the hands of those who love, understand and work within it'. This could never be achieved if the principal authority was staffed by civil servants.

Margaret Meades retired at the end of 1979 and Tristram Ricketts was duly promoted to take her place, and at last Sir Desmond Plummer had the man of his choice as his unfettered assistant. It was noticeable that his appointment provoked the only press comment that I can recall on Levy Board staffing when on 6 July 1979 the *Sporting Chronicle*, on congratulating Tristram, stated,

> I do, however, wonder a little about the Board's methods of recruitment. And I am just a little uneasy about what could be seen as an extension of Chairman Sir Desmond Plummer's already considerable power. For although Ricketts joined the Levy Board in March 1974, and has been Deputy Secretary for the last three years, it is less well known that he also served with Sir Desmond when the latter was Chairman of the GLC, and that he made the move from politics to racing politics at Sir Desmond's invitation. It is my view, though, that a position of such importance should have been advertised.

Of course the *Sporting Chronicle* was right, but why had there never been any comment on the whole series of 'introductions' since the departure of Rupert Brazier-Creagh?

By the time of his appointment Tristram Ricketts was an authority on all aspects of racing administration and his dedication and common sense were to steer the Levy Board in a much more positive direction until his move to the British Horseracing Board in 1993. Sir Desmond retired on 30 September 1982 and was succeeded by Sir Ian Trethowan.

There had also been changes to our home circumstances. Our only son, Charles, had been born in 1969 when we moved from London to Ardleigh where we lived until we moved to the Old Vicarage in Leavenheath on 16 March 1978, where we have remained. We have loved living in Suffolk and this was to be a help to me when I finally worked for the Suffolk Red Cross.

CHAPTER 12

The Horserace Betting Levy Board – A Different Atmosphere
1982-1991

MANY YEARS LATER, on 5 November 1990, Tristram Ricketts told me that it took the whole of Sir Desmond Plummer's period of office (eight years) to restore a proper relationship between the Board and the Jockey Club. Tristram was never one to exaggerate or to comment without good reason, and it is hard so long after the events to recognize how desperate the situation had become. I did not agree with Tristram that relationships were fully restored and this was largely because of the difference in submissions to the Royal Commission on Gambling. Sir Desmond, for all his joviality, was not really a racing man. Unlike his two successors, he could not be described as being interested in horses, and he was much too concerned about his own public image. It became something of a joke to see him each year on Grand National Day endeavouring to place himself in front of the cameras in the unsaddling enclosure after the great race at Aintree. Things had indeed become easier but it was really during the Chairmanship of Sir Ian Trethowan that the Board and the Jockey Club once more worked together amicably for the benefit of the industry which they served.

My battles were now well and truly over and I was able to enjoy my work for my remaining nine years in exactly the

The Horserace Betting Levy Board Staff, 1983.

The Horserace Betting Levy Board, 1987.

Front row, left to right: Sir Nevil Macready, Sir Patrick Meaney, Sir Ian Trethowan (Chairman), Lord Wyatt of Weeford, Sir Thomas Pilkington. Back row, left to right: D.M. Stewart, I.G. Stevenson, R.L. Brack, M.E. Wates, R.T. Ricketts (Chief Executive), L.P. Cowburn, the author, A. Bruce, I.F.C. Beresford.

same way as I had done when I first joined in 1963. I had no ambition beyond providing the best service for the various interests with which I was concerned. I had long realized that I would never be the Chief Executive and I did not have the inclination to be involved with all the permanent infighting which appears to be a hallmark of racing politics. The responsibilities of the Board are wide and there was ample reward in looking after so many good people who were totally dependent on us for their survival. The longer I was with the Board the more involved I became with the veterinary research workers, the farriers and the breed societies. When another executive was made redundant by Sir Ian Trethowan, I took over some of the responsibilities for the Horseracing Forensic Laboratory and the Horserace Anti-Doping Committee, and I was pleased when in 1985 I was given the assistance of Ian Beresford who was to work happily with me until I retired in 1991.

The work with the Board's Veterinary Advisory Committee had always been all absorbing. The Board can take credit for some of the dramatic advances which have been made in equine research over the last forty years. We were fortunate to have the assistance of able men like Sir John Ritchie, Sir David Evans, Sir William Henderson and Professor Lord Soulsby (the first veterinarian to become a Member of the House of Lords) who were widely admired by the profession they served. We made regular visits to the Animal Health Trust and the six university veterinary schools to monitor the work which we supported and we organized conferences every five years to present the results of the studies to owners, trainers and breeders. It was certainly encouraging to me to know that there were no complaints throughout my entire service of this aspect of the

Board's administration. It even came back to me that Sir Ian Trethowan became irritated by the number of people who paid tribute to my work, but he, of course, was largely unaware of the circumstances which prevailed in earlier years. The truth is that the investment made by the Board, particularly in young emerging scientists, enabled some of them to become world leaders in their chosen disciplines.

I had recognized from my earliest visit to Cambridge University Veterinary School in 1963 how frustrating it was for enthusiastic scientists, who wanted to undertake studies on horses but could not do so because so little money was available. The arrival of the Levy Board, with its annual grant in aid of equine veterinary science and equine veterinary education, was to make a huge difference, and I became the Board's regular link with the British Equine Veterinary Association which had been formed in 1961 through the initiatives of John Hickman, Michael Hunt, Peter Rossdale, Leo Mahaffey, Ian Silver and Alistair Fraser, all of whom were to contribute substantially to the scientific advances which were to be made in all the principal disciplines. I admired the dedication of the research workers and I could see how important it was that they should have someone with whom they could communicate who would, so to speak, be on their side. My military training had taught me the futility of unnecessary bureaucracy and I was determined that this aspect of the Board's affairs would be run entirely for the benefit of the people for whom the money was intended. I was fortunate that even during my worst moments there was no interference with the work of the Board's Veterinary Advisory Committee. Those who were against me did not understand it, and the Committee themselves recognized that I did everything I could to promote their initiatives.

Two letters, in particular, gave me great pleasure, and these are reproduced below:

From the President of the British Equine Veterinary Association, Dr P.D. Rossdale

16 December 1976

Dear Martin,

At the 64th Meeting of our Executive Committee, held at BVA Headquarters on 14th December, the question of equine veterinary research was raised; and during the discussion a member spoke of the diligent service that you had devoted to this cause. Subsequently there was spontaneous support for a suggestion that we, the Executive Committee, should convey our appreciation of your work, and it was resolved that:

'The President should write to Mr Martin Crawshay, Secretary to the Veterinary Advisory Panel of the Horserace Betting Levy Board and express the unanimous gratitude of the Executive Committee of the British Equine Veterinary Association for the service he has given to equine veterinary research in the UK; and for the friendly, helpful and constructive manner in which he has performed his duties.'

It was further minuted that:

'The Secretary of BEVA should keep Mr Crawshay informed of the Annual Programme of the Association and that Mr Crawshay should be made aware that he would be welcomed as a guest at any part of that programme he might wish to attend; thus strengthening the bridge of good relations which has been formed between BEVA and the Horserace Betting Levy Board in recent years.'

It gives me, personally, great pleasure to undertake the task of writing to you as my year of office draws to a close. As a practitioner, I am particularly conscious of the debt that all members of my profession owe to those who devote their energies to research, thereby helping to advance the frontiers of the art and science we practise. Those, such as yourself, who help members of our profession to help themselves play no less a part than those who actually engage in the research itself.

I thought it proper that I should send a copy of this letter to the Chairman of your Board.

Yours sincerely,
Peter D. Rossdale.

From Dr A.C. Fraser

5th April 1978

Dear Martin

On my retirement from the Board's Veterinary Advisory Committee I feel that I must once again express my gratitude to you for your friendly and efficient organization of the Committee's affairs and I fully appreciate the unstinted expenditure of your time and application, often in the face of considerable difficulties, which have smoothed the Committee's path.

As you are aware I have thoroughly enjoyed being a member of what I feel should rightly be called your committee and I gratefully attribute to yourself a large share of responsibility for its happy blend of camaraderie and scientific application.

With very best wishes, yours sincerely,
A.C. Fraser

Presenting a Levy Board premium to Mr Jim Salt, owner of the Supreme Champion at the National Shire Horse Stallion Show, 1983.

Presenting a trophy to Miss Sydney Smith at the National Hackney Breed Show, 1989.

Letters such as these were all the more welcome because the writers really had no idea of just how difficult the circumstances had been, and many people reading this book will become aware for the very first time of the prejudice and mismanagement which prevailed for so long.

I was equally fortunate in my relationships with representatives of the breed societies and the Worshipful Company of Farriers whose interests I looked after for twenty-eight years.

It was agreed that I would retire on 31 July 1991 and I was grateful to Tristram Ricketts for an increase in salary and his assurance that the Board would base my pension on service until I was 65. This was entirely satisfactory and I was pleased that he had always recognized my contribution to the Board's affairs and did what he could to make up for what had happened in earlier years. Tristram was a master tactician but the internecine warfare was to test even his ability to the limits. My guess is that he enjoyed working with Sir Ian Trethowan more than he did with Sir Desmond Plummer. Sir Ian Trethowan was a relaxed individual who had confidence in his staff and he once told me that his job as Chairman would have been about perfect were it not for the constant arguments with the bookmakers. This is not a history of the Levy Board, but a record of the negotiations with the bookmakers would be interesting reading. The very composition of the Board with its responsibilities to the Government meant that it left no stone unturned in efforts to reach agreement with those who produced the levy. Nevertheless, in my service of twenty-eight years, sixteen levy schemes were agreed, six were 'imposed' by the Home Office-appointed Members and five were referred to the Home Secretary for determination. The arguments, of course, continue to this day.

Grania and I were appreciative of the arrangements which were made by so many to mark my retirement. The last three months were taken up with teaching my able successor, Libby Archer, who did not arrive until 24 June, and saying goodbye to the many friends with whom I had worked so happily for so many years. Whatever the atmosphere inside the office, the negotiations outside had mostly been amicable and successful. It is not possible to mention everyone by name but nearly every organization did something to thank me for whatever contribution I had made to their affairs. I was to be President of the National Pony Society in 1992 and President of the British Percheron

At the Levy Board office, 1991.

Horse Society in 1993 and most of the other societies made me an Honorary Member. I was particularly honoured to be invited to become an Honorary Member of the British Equine Veterinary Association at their Annual General Meeting on 12 December 1990 and to be invited by John Owen, President of the Association, to become a Trustee of the BEVA Trust in July 1991. These were particularly rewarding as they were to keep me in touch with affairs in which I had been interested for so long. The Racecourse Association gave Grania and me badges for life which entitle us to free entry to almost every racecourse in the United Kingdom. In December 1991 I was admitted to the Livery of the Worshipful Company of Farriers. I had been the Board's officer overseeing grants to the Company throughout my service which had provided for assistance in education and training of apprentice farriers.

Sir John Sparrow and the Levy Board gave me a 'Retirement Dinner' at the Stafford Hotel on 25 July to which I invited Peter Rossdale, who had done so much to foster the good relations I had with so many equine vets, as my personal guest. I was pleased that my speech, which made no reference to matters which had been laid to rest and which did not concern Members in 1991, found particular favour with Woodrow Wyatt, Chairman of the Tote, who had always been a loyal supporter of my 'fringe activities' and who congratulated me afterwards. Praise from an established politician was praise indeed. (A copy of this speech is included as an Appendix.) I gave my own lunch for the Levy Board staff a few days before I left and I was so pleased that it had once again become the happy organization which any group of thirty people working together ought to be.

My final, and perhaps my greatest, reward was the retirement dinner at the Jockey Club in Newmarket on 2 August, to which Grania and I were both invited. This was organized by Professor Twink Allen and Dr Jenny Mumford, and was attended by many colleagues from Newmarket. I had known, and I hope helped, Twink and Jenny over many years. Both had excelled in their respective fields and were highly respected in scientific and equine circles. I had remembered Peter Burrell, former Director of the National Stud, who came to the dinner, coming to the

Levy Board in 1963 and saying, in reference to Twink, 'This is a man whom you must support'. We did indeed support him, and continuously over many years (Twink was then head of the TBA Equine Fertility Unit and later Professor of Equine Reproduction at Cambridge University.) Jenny had been a research worker under Walter Plowright at the Royal Veterinary College and had been chosen by Brian Singleton, when Director of the Animal Health Trust, to establish the Equine Virology Unit at that organization. Jenny subsequently became Head of the Department of Infectious Diseases and then Director of Science at the Trust. This was a very enjoyable occasion in lovely surroundings which I will always remember. It gave Grania and me great pleasure when, on 17 May 1992, we were able to entertain a number of veterinary and breed society friends for lunch at our home in Leavenheath and so say a personal thank you to them for all that they had done for us.

Thus did my work for the Horserace Betting Levy Board come to an end, and at 63 I was still full of energy, so what was I to do?

CHAPTER 13

The Suffolk Red Cross and Other Charitable Work
1991-2000

I HAD HARDLY LEFT the Levy Board before I was invited by Belinda Somerleyton to assist her in her work for the Suffolk Red Cross. Belinda had joined the Red Cross shortly after her marriage in 1963 and had been President of the Suffolk Branch since 1983. According to Belinda I had asked her if she might have a job for me in retirement, but be that as it may, I accepted her offer to become a Trustee of the Suffolk Red Cross and to take responsibility for reorganizing the Open Gardens Scheme. I had been an established friend of both Bill and Belinda for many years and I welcomed the opportunity to work in Suffolk where I had lived, albeit as a commuter, since 1978. I brought with me Michael Tollemache as another Trustee who much looked forward to opening his garden at Tollemache Hall which he had created from nothing since 1966, and Christopher Robinson who was to be the principal organizer of the Fund Raising Committee for both East and West Suffolk. Both were to be invaluable additions to the Suffolk team. The arrangement was that I would be solely responsible for the Garden Scheme as a volunteer for up to five years.

I was delighted to be given a free hand to reorganize the Garden Scheme. Although the scheme had been established for many years it had never achieved its potential and for a

At Home, 1997.

number of reasons was unsuccessful. Suffolk is a large county with many magnificent gardens and it should have been a leader in the county league table. It was in fact tenth leading county in 1991 and raised under £3,000 for the charity. I soon discovered that garden owners were disenchanted with the organization of the Scheme and were withdrawing faster than they were coming in.

Garden opening was, and still is, a growth activity. Everyone loves gardens and gardening is one of the few activities in which there are no 'antis'. I knew at once that this was something in which I would become interested and I resolved to make sure that Suffolk would soon be a leader in this field.

The Red Cross is a massive organization and in 1991 was run entirely on a county basis. Suffolk has some eighteen 'centres' and each centre has its own organizer and volunteers, and all centres are responsible to Branch Headquarters in Bury St Edmunds. Branch Headquarters has its own staff under a Director who was then responsible to the President and Trustees, who themselves were responsible to National Headquarters in London. Each centre provides a series of services such as provision for medical loan facilities, escort duties and first aid cover, and each centre is also involved in fund-raising. The Branch Director at that time was an ex-policeman who was much respected and was referred to by everyone as Mr Wakerell. I found him easy to work with and it was soon apparent that both he and Belinda were only too pleased to leave all the arrangements for garden opening to me.

I made a fresh start from 1992 and increased the number of participating gardens. My first task was to stop any more owners from withdrawing. I had certain advantages. I was about the same age as most garden owners and I was able to promise them that the only person they would have to deal with was me. I gave assurances that their wishes would be respected and that supporting staff would be available where required. I visited all the gardens and managed to persuade nearly all of them to provide the teas, which was a great help to local Red Cross volunteers. Teas are an important part of garden opening and visitors like to settle down and enjoy the local surroundings. Most open days are on a Sunday and it is a typical pastime to get under the trees in someone else's garden and enjoy the sort of teas which our countrymen have been producing for generations. The message went round that I was taking my responsibilities seriously and the number of participating gardens increased steadily year by year. On one occasion I received a letter from an owner in

With Christopher Whybrow and Toby at a Red Cross garden, 2000.

the morning declining to open, but on meeting his wife in the afternoon, I managed to persuade her to countermand his instructions.

I found myself fully absorbed in organizing what was so obviously a worthwhile activity which brought pleasure to many and useful money to a worthy charity. Everyone was helpful and I found that everyone was on the same side, which was a contrast to the many opposing camps in the horse world. Suffolk soon climbed the county league table to third place and steadily increased its total takings and average per garden. My previous experience in looking after some fifty veterinary research workers was exactly what was required for an equal number of hesitant garden owners who might have been frightened by possible burglars.

Belinda decided to step down as President at the end of 1996 after thirteen years in that position, and was subsequently awarded the OBE for her outstanding contribution to the Suffolk charity. I had been much impressed by her calm response to many hideous difficulties and by her willingness to undertake whatever duty presented itself. Her power of persuasion was her secret weapon and one of the Trustees was quite right in saying that no one likes to say no to Belinda. Belinda was succeeded by Sophia van den Arend who had been helping me with the gardens and who filled the vacancy with as much dedication and enthusiasm as her predecessor. I realized how lucky Suffolk was to have two such able personalities who, despite large families and other responsibilities, gave so much time and dedication to the Red Cross. I could have retired at this point but I decided to stay on as I was much enjoying myself and I wanted to give as much help to Sophia as I had to Belinda.

The arrangements for administering the Red Cross were to change dramatically from January 1998 when the charity was reorganized on a national basis, which resulted in the abolition of the county structure and the Trustees. From 1 January 1998 all money raised was to be passed to Regional Headquarters which, in our case was Eastern Region in Northampton, and this meant that money raised by Suffolk could no longer all be spent by Suffolk in Suffolk as had always applied in the past. This new procedure was supposed to be more administratively convenient and more economical, but was bitterly opposed by most of the long-serving volunteers; however it had to be accepted. The extra layer of bureaucracy was undoubtedly cumbersome and resulted in additional travelling and meetings. Most of the

The author (second from left) at the awards ceremony arranged by the National Blood Service at the University Arms Hotel, Cambridge, 23 August 2001.

Suffolk Trustees stayed on as Members of the new Branch Council but they felt undervalued and rather impotent as they were now only engaged in an advisory capacity and had no executive responsibilities whatever. The new structure was not successful and in late 2001 the charity was re-organized for a second time on the basis of areas. Suffolk was merged with Cambridgeshire and Norfolk into one area, and it is hoped that the new proposals will be more acceptable than the previous ones. Fund-raising is hard work and those involved like to feel that the money raised is spent on the purpose of the charity rather than on administration. In the case of Suffolk we felt we were providing many excellent services in the county for disadvantaged people and we took pride in what we saw as a successful and economical enterprise.

I continued to organize the Open Gardens Scheme without impediment for a further four years until I retired at the end of the season in the year 2000. I had done it for nine years, which was longer than I had originally intended, but I had much enjoyed working with many like-minded and delightful people all of whom were proud to be associated with the Red Cross. By the time I retired we were making over £25,000 a year for the charity, but nothing I did could have been achieved without the help I received from Grania and from all those at every level who worked with me for the benefit of the Red Cross. Perhaps what gave me as much pleasure as anything was the fact that I raised over £2,000 over the years by selling the golf balls which my dog, Toby, and I found during our afternoon walks round the edge of Stoke-by-Nayland golf course. During my nine years the Open Gardens Scheme raised some £175,000 for the Red Cross. I was pleased to be awarded my Badge of Honour in March 1997 for my service to the Red Cross by Mrs Elspeth Thomas, the Chairman of the Council, and Grania was equally pleased to receive a Special Certificate of Appreciation from the County President, Sophia van den Arend in September 2000. We certainly felt that our work had been recognized and it had all been enormously worth while.

In addition to working for the Red Cross I did other charitable work for the Home of Rest for Horses with which I had been associated since 1979, and for ten years I was also Treasurer of the Leavenheath Parochial Church Council. There did not seem to be any spare time in retirement and I counted myself lucky to be so fully involved in useful activities.

Finally, I record one other organization with which I was associated over many years. At the suggestion of my mother I became a blood donor while serving with the 65th Training Regiment, Royal Armoured Corps, at Catterick in 1955. I continued to give blood at least twice a year until I was compulsorily retired in 1997 after making 83 donations; enough to fill more than two army jerry cans each of which would contain 4½ gallons. I was both surprised and delighted to accept with Grania an invitation from the National Blood Service to a dinner which was held on 23 August 2001 at the University Arms Hotel in Cambridge, where those who had donated at least 75 pints of blood were entertained and each given a crystal plate in recognition of their support for the service. Only 2 per cent of donors actually achieve 75 pints or more. I was always pleased to be one of the 6 per cent of the eligible population who contributed to the 10,000 units of blood which are needed every day. Contributing to the National Blood Service is something we should all try to do rather than leave it to someone else.

Chapter 14

Reflections

Now that I am enjoying my twilight years it is inevitable that I should reflect on the vast changes to every aspect of life in the last seventy years. My own life has been, and still is, determined by my experiences of the Second World War. I did not have to fight but I was 11 when the war broke out and 17 when it ended and I followed every aspect until the unconditional surrender of Germany and Japan. Every day now I read the obituaries of those whose distinguished service was recognized in some way or other and whose contribution ensured that almost alone in Europe we were never an occupied country, and that the United Kingdom ended that war respected the world over. It could be argued that our contribution between 1939 and 1945 was the greatest of any nation since records began. No one would dispute the unity of the country and the singleness of purpose which made every one of us proud of our national identity.

Some decline was inevitable, but those who gave so much would be forgiven for asking whether their sacrifice was worth while. The remainder of the twentieth century appears to me to have been downhill all the way, and I find it difficult to be optimistic about the future. While there have been major advances towards the elimination of poverty, the poverty of my youth has been replaced by ignorance and the worst excesses of materialism. Real values have been eroded

In South Africa, 1992.

Richard's Aunt Betty, the author, Richard Gisborough and Toby Chalonor in South Africa, 1992.

and standards have been in decline in every aspect of human behaviour. Tony Blair, as Prime Minister designate, was totally correct to specify 'Education, Education, Education' before he came to power in 1997, but the question is, what does he mean by that word? In spite of condemnation by politicians over a quarter of a century, the 'yob' culture reigns supreme. State education in many areas is behind what it was before the outbreak of the First World War and ignorance prevails in many areas relating to history, culture and religion. Many of the young are totally disadvantaged without being aware of their disadvantages.

The pursuit of equality for all is largely a waste of time, and how dull life would be if we were indeed all equal. Every child should be encouraged to develop his or her own personality to its best advantage and superstars will only emerge if they are segregated and given the necessary specialist training from the earliest age possible. Until recently the principal voluntary organizations were run by families of status who, recognizing their good fortune, wanted to pay something back to those less fortunate than themselves, but *noblesse oblige* as it was called, is now sidelined and as someone said to me recently, 'they don't want people like us any more'. The result is that many excellent people no longer put themselves forward and replacements are often rather too interested in what can be claimed by way of expenses. Even as late as 1964, John Morrison, later Lord Margadale, served as Member of Parliament for Salisbury without drawing the salary. It is very sad that that sort of example and service, which used to be commonplace, has totally disappeared.

The blame for so much of which we disapprove rests entirely with ourselves. People are afraid to speak out on many subjects which matter most for fear of contradiction from pressure groups representing those who want to alter our entire national identity. The failure of politicians and above all our church leaders to confront those who promote political correctness has done untold damage to the moral fibre of the country, and has done much to hasten our real decline. The question should be asked, 'What is political correctness anyway?' Things are either correct or not correct and political correctness is a matter of opinion. Successive church leaders have stood on the sidelines as one by one the rules of sexual behaviour, which have prevailed for generations, have been broken to satisfy the desires of an ever more decadent society. The prison population and the number of unmarried mothers continue to rise inexorably; they are not unrelated but the authorities and the so-called professionals cannot bear to face the truth.

The result of giving in to pressures from those who appear to derive pleasure from condemning everything which previous generations held sacred has been an ever-increasing surge in juvenile crime, litter and vandalism. Few people believe a word from Government or the police on crime reduction but recognize that they have little chance in the event of any encounter with the most undesirable elements of society. Most people believe, and have believed for over thirty years, that too many criminals go unpunished and that the whole legal process is weighted in favour of the wrong-doers.

The blame for so much of our malaise is directed at parents without recognizing that those parents themselves were unfit to bring up children. The disease has been with us for so long that it has become endemic and cannot be cured without a new approach which condemns wrong-

Playing croquet with Charlie, 1992.

doing and refuses to accept excuses. Any cure is bound to be painful and will result in some unfairness, but the blame for that will rest with those who have failed to speak out in the past. The need is for a concentration on the Ten Commandments, which should by law be posted prominently in every primary school, and for the promotion of marriage which should be restored to its rightful place as the ideal basis for the upbringing of children. The first political or church leader who identifies with these suggestions could well be the one to whom we turn for a moral revival. Half measures simply will not do.

I myself recognize how fortunate I have been. The important things happened at the right time; my first house, the job which suited me so well and the person whom I

With Lennox Hannay at Spring Hill, 1993.

married. For a man there are three things which really matter; job, home and marriage, and if all three are going well you are extremely lucky. I have been fortunate in my friends, most of whom have been established for many years. Some of the happiest moments came in later life with two particular parties which I organized.

The first was for Grania's sixtieth birthday when I secretly invited her friends from the past to a dinner in her honour at the Cavalry and Guards Club. The first that Grania knew about it was when she walked in to the club to find so many friends awaiting her. The second was the party for my seventieth birthday, also at the Cavalry and Guards Club, when almost everyone invited was available to attend. Two interesting points about this second party were, first, that almost everyone (apart from my son Charles and his eventual bride-to-be Antonia Ward) had been a friend before I met Grania and second, that, by chance, there were no second husbands or wives. It has been very nice for us that nearly all our friends have remained together, and we who have stayed the course have benefited so much from an enduring marriage.

Time has gone too fast but there is always something useful to do. I have made my mistakes and it is interesting that gambling on horses led me to the Levy Board so that the bookmakers eventually paid my pension. I destroyed my 'betting book' so that it should never be found and I am thankful that Charles has shown no inclination to go down that road. As someone once said to me, 'If you have not done anything wrong in your life, you have lived a very dull life'. Perhaps a secret of life is not to worry too much as a solution will usually be found. Lennox Hannay had some useful advice written and framed behind his bed in his room at Eton. It said, 'Today is the Tomorrow you worried about Yesterday and all is well'. Rien ne va plus.

Appendix I

Case History
Submitted to Sir Denys Hicks,
Deputy Chairman, on 12 July 1972

I JOINED THE STAFF of the Horserace Betting Levy Board in March 1963 in the post of Deputy Assistant Secretary (Schemes and Projects). The post had been advertised and I was interviewed by Sir Rupert Brazier-Creagh (then Secretary of the Levy Board) and by Mr B.H. Catchpole (then Assistant Secretary (Finance)). I was chosen from a total of 12 persons interviewed, and I had immediately previously been on a short-list for a position of Stewards' Secretary with Weatherbys. I had been trying to obtain a job in racing for about two years since leaving the Army where I had done a certain amount of race riding in Germany.

I understood at the time of my interview that the reason for my appointment was twofold, firstly because the Board was about to assume responsibility for the National Stud and secondly because the Board had agreed that the then Assistant Secretary (Schemes and Projects), Brigadier O.G. Brooke, would be serving only on the basis of being present two days a week.

From the outset my responsibilities included the Secretaryship of the Veterinary Advisory Committee, matters connected with the National Stud, prize money and related subjects, and modernisation schemes and improvements to racecourses.

This arrangement worked very satisfactorily until the unfortunate departure of Brigadier Brooke in December 1963 as a result of ill-health. In January 1964 it was decided between Lord Harding (then Chairman of the Levy Board) and Sir Rupert Brazier-Creagh that no replacement was required for Brigadier Brooke and that matters which had previously been referred to him would in future be dealt with by me in my capacity as Deputy Assistant Secretary. A circular letter dated 27th January 1964 was duly sent to all racecourses to this effect.

In July 1964 we were informed by the Secretary that, owing to a great increase in the pressure of work, two additional executives would join the staff in August, one in the capacity of Deputy Secretary (Plans) to replace Brigadier Brooke, and the other in the capacity of Assistant Secretary (Finance).

The proposed increase in the number of executives came as a considerable surprise and the existing executives were not convinced of the necessity. The reason for at least one of the appointments was different from what had been represented. I myself told the Secretary that I did not think additional executives were necessary when racing with him at an evening meeting at Kempton Park, but to no avail.

The next day the Secretary came to see me in my office to inform me of the exact nature of his proposed appointment of a Deputy Secretary (Plans), as he duly realised that such an appointment would inevitably have some effect on my position with the Board. Since this was a conversation of extreme importance to my position I remember it in great detail.

The Secretary gave me assurances that the appointment was entirely to deal with additional work, and that I would continue to do all that I had been doing up until that time. He said that I would continue to have direct access to himself on all matters with which I was concerned, and the emphasis of the discussion was to allay any fears that I might have that my work would be taken on by someone else.

At this meeting I told the Secretary that if there was any question of my not having come up to the required standard, or of having disappointed in any way, I would offer my resignation to the Board. I said that I would prefer to know at once if any failing on my part was the cause of the decision to recruit additional executives. I was told that this was definitely not so and that there was no question of my having failed to meet the necessary requirement. I made the same points to Mr Catchpole who had now been appointed Deputy Secretary (Finance) and received similar assurances.

Despite these assurances and regardless of who the new Deputy Secretary would be I realised that the new appointment was bound to affect my position, and however rigidly the assurances were adhered to at the beginning, time would eventually erode them.

Mr Victory joined the staff in August 1964 as Deputy Secretary (Plans) and since he had no knowledge or experience of racing it was agreed that he and I should share an office in order that I might provide him with day to day assistance.

Sir Rupert Brazier-Creagh resigned as Secretary to the Levy Board in June 1965 partly on doctor's advice and also because of his personal commitments in Ireland. His departure was a serious blow to the Levy Board and a problem arose over his replacement.

Obviously the two Deputy Secretaries, Mr Catchpole and

Mr Victory were the two members of the existing staff who were considered for the vacancy. However, it was decided to advertise the position in the National Press and there was therefore a likelihood that the replacement would be found from outside.

The repercussions of such an appointment, (that is to say from an outside source), were bound to be sufficiently far reaching, following the increases which had so recently been made, that the Board could hardly have taken into account the internal circumstances surrounding the existing staff. If the appointment had be made from outside it obviously meant that neither of the two Deputy Secretaries was considered of sufficient standing for the post, and that therefore the Assistant Secretaries would also be denied an obvious opportunity for promotion.

I felt that it was imperative that this point should be represented to the Chairman together with the fact that there were already too many executive posts for the amount of work available. With the change of policy (cessation of breeding) on the National Stud and the fact that many of the Board's schemes were now established, it had become evident that seven full time executives, including one Accountant, could not be justified. I realised that my own position was vulnerable and that in the interests of everyone, the Board included, that proper representation should be made before consideration was given to filling the vacant appointment of Secretary.

I made my representations to Sir Rupert Brazier-Creagh on 11th June and to Lord Harding on 15th June 1965. Both told me that I was right to have said what I did, and Lord Harding was sufficiently impressed to send for me the next day to specifically thank me for my initiative. At this time I did not mention this initiative to any other member of the staff for very obvious reasons.

Brigadier H.J. de W. Waller was appointed Secretary to the Levy Board in October 1965. Shortly before the announcement of the appointment Lord Harding had informed the executives when they were called together in the Board Room, and he had then said, realising the implications, 'No one here need fear for his job'. By this time much of the work which I had been doing had been taken over by Mr Victory and it was not long before the new Secretary realised the problem that existed in the office arising from insufficient work to justify the employment of the existing executives.

What went on behind the scenes remains a mystery but on 3rd January 1966 the Secretary sent for me and said that it had been decided to make my post of Assistant Secretary (Plans) redundant and that I was therefore being given three months notice. He was obviously very embarrassed and added that 'it had to be me because I was unmarried and had some private means'. The interview was followed up by a letter the next day.

In view of everything that had led up to this decision I was completely staggered, and my feelings were not lessened by the Secretary's supporting reasons. I saw Lord Harding the same morning and reminded him of my previous interview and that he himself had said only three months earlier that 'no one here need fear for his job.' His only reply was that he was sorry but that he had to take the Secretary's advice. He added that I could if I wished make an appeal to the Board.

I have always assumed that the reason for so abrupt a dismissal stemmed from Lord Harding's and Brigadier

Waller's belief that they could easily find me another job in racing whereas this would not have been easy for any of the others. This belief is strengthened by the wording in my letter of dismissal. The notice of dismissal was however withdrawn after ten days, following the resignation of another executive, Mr J.B. Hay. It will be appreciated that the build-up to all these events had a profoundly unsettling effect on such a small organisation.

Lord Wigg became Chairman of the Levy Board in November 1967, and no particular staff matters arose until the appointment of Mr McKenna as an Assistant Secretary in July 1968.

The relevant extract from the Minutes of the meeting of the Board on 15th July 1968 reads as follows:

> The Board was informed that the Secretary, in consultation with Mr Hambro and Sir Alexander Sim, had offered the post of Assistant Secretary to Mr R. McKenna, a Treasury Official. Mr McKenna had accepted the post and hoped to join in September. Lord Wigg pointed out that should any redundancy be necessary in future amongst the executive staff, Mr McKenna would, under the terms of the Fulton Report, be able to return to the Treasury. Since there had been a reduction in staff once before, he felt that there was an important advantage in recognising this fact. He also wished to assure those at present in the service of the Board that their positions would not be placed in jeopardy should redundancy occur in the future.

At the meeting on 21st October 1968 the Board resolved that an organisation and methods survey of the Levy Board headquarters should be carried out by the Economist Intelligence Unit. This investigation was carried out and the Economist Intelligence Unit duly reported in February 1969.

The Report of the Economist Intelligence Unit was considered by the Board at a special meeting on 28th February 1969 and it was at this meeting that it was decided that Brigadier Waller should be succeeded by Mr Victory as Secretary of the Board.

The Report of the Economist Intelligence Unit recommended four executive posts other than the Secretary and the Accountant and in view of my length of service I anticipated being offered the post of Assistant Principal Officer (Administration) or the Executive Officer (Racecourse Improvements). I had in fact been carrying much of the responsibility listed under these two appointments since I had first joined the staff of the Board and I had had plenty of experience in both fields.

Brigadier Waller invited me to go along to his house on the evening of 3rd March 1969 to discuss with him my future in the light of the EIU recommendations. He already knew of his own imminent departure, and it therefore came as a considerable shock to me when he said 'clearly I was to lose my job following the EIU report'. In view of earlier events already described and in view of Lord Wigg's assurances following Mr McKenna's appointment a move of this nature seemed incomprehensible. I said that I did not at all understand why 'clearly I was to lose my job'. Brigadier Waller talked to me that evening for about half an hour. I said very little as he was obviously under the Chairman's instructions. He said he thought 'I ought to be moving on' and that I need do nothing as 'another job would be found for me'. He agreed that I had given very good service to him and to the Board, but said that it would be better if I did not refer to the previous occasion of redundancy or any assurances which had been given. At this juncture I did not dispute anything the Brigadier said as it was obvious that he was going to report back to the Chairman. The implication was clear enough. The Chairman wanted me to go quietly and he would find me something he considered suitable but I must not say anything.

On 6th March 1969 the Chairman called me into his office and asked me why I had not asked him any questions about my future in the light of the EIU Report. I replied that I thought it was for him to raise the matter but that it was my hope that I would be offered one of the two jobs that still remained to be filled. There followed a long tirade to the effect that I was unsuitable for either job as I would not be able to manage them. Nevertheless of the nineteen duties listed under the Principal Officer (Administration) on page 69 of the Report I had been dealing with items one to fifteen inclusive and without complaint since I joined the Board.

There was no point whatsoever in arguing and the upshot was that the Chairman eventually said that 'he was prepared to keep me' without specifying what I was to do. Whereas the other executives received salary increases arising out of the Report my salary was pegged at the figure of £2,625 and the Chairman specifically ruled out the increment of £125 to which I was entitled on 25th March 1969. This was the first occasion which the Chairman discriminated against me on the subject of pay.

On 24th March 1969 the Chairman wrote to me informing me that the Board had decided to adopt the Executive Structure as recommended in the EIU Report and that the Salary Structure proposed would be effective with effect from 1st January 1969. I did not participate in the revised salary structure despite having already completed six years service, and the Chairman's decision was that I would be 'on probation' for six months. No reasons were given. Nevertheless I continued to carry out identical work to what I had already been doing and I was given the title of 'Assistant Principal Officer'. The probationary period came to an end without incident in September 1969 when my salary was revised in line with the EIU recommendations.

On 15th April 1970 the Chairman called me into his office and said that he was making certain changes to the Executive Staff so as to make them interchangeable with the Civil Service. He said that he proposed bringing in Miss Meades from the Home Office, and that he proposed making a change in my position so that I would become the 'Executive Officer' which would be a new post, but that there would be no change in my salary.

I was asked whether I agreed with what was proposed for me, but since I had no indication of what was proposed other than what is written in the previous paragraph I said that I did.

On 17th April when I saw the papers for the Board meeting on 20th April 1970 I realised that I had not been told that whereas my salary was to remain unchanged, the salaries of all the other executives were to be considerably increased and this was to smooth the introduction of Miss Meades.

I realised that the Chairman had deceived me, since, at my interview on 15th April, he had said nothing about Miss Meades coming in above me nor had he mentioned that the other executives were to receive salary increases. This was the second occasion on which the Chairman discriminated against me on the subject of pay.

I expected that Lord Wigg would inform the Board at the

meeting on 20th April that 'I had raised no objection' to the new proposals, and in view of the circumstances I informed one of the Board Members by telephone on 19th April.

At the meeting on 15th February 1971 the Board approved a general review of salaries in the light of the rise in the cost of living index, as a result of which increases were awarded as follows:-

    Executives $3\frac{1}{2}$%
    Remainder of the Staff   8%

The lower rate of increase for the executives was to allow for the very substantial increases which had been awarded during the summer of 1970 following the arrival of Miss Meades, but I alone was excluded from the increases which were then awarded.

In a letter dated 16th February 1971 I was duly informed of my salary increase with effect from 1st January 1971 amounting to $3\frac{1}{2}$%. In effect this meant that I alone among the entire regular staff of the Board had been denied an 8% salary increase since 1st January 1970 while nearly all of the executives had had even more than that. My information was that as far as Lord Wigg was concerned this was intentional, but I wondered whether this peculiarity was known to the Board.

On 26th February 1971 I approached the Chairman about the $3\frac{1}{2}$% cost of living rise in the light of the 8% approved by the Board for the staff. He said he would look at my position again, but on 2nd March he called me in to his office to say that I had been treated identically with the other executives and that the $3\frac{1}{2}$% cost of living increase was correct. He added that I was only 'attached to the staff'. This was the third occasion on which the Chairman discriminated against me on the subject of pay.

On 19th July 1971 the Board approved further salary increases both for the executives and for the staff. The increase for the executives was approximately 10% but for the staff was small. The appropriate resolution of the Board Minutes says 'That the recommendations of the Staff Establishment Committee at paragraph 4, 10 and 12 of paper LB/P(71)193, dated 8th July 1971, be adopted'.

I discovered afterwards that there had been no meeting of the Staff Establishment Committee.

Once more I was excluded from any salary increase and I therefore wrote to Lord Wigg on 22nd July 1971 asking if I might be given the reason for the omission on this occasion.

I received a reply from Mr Massey on the same day after an interview with Lord Wigg, in which I was informed that my post as Executive Officer was not one which had a relationship with a Civil Service grade and that my salary was only adjustable at the time of the annual review based on rises in the cost of living. The fact that my position alone was selected for isolation was emphasised by the decision of the Board at the meeting on 20th September 1971 to increase the salary of the Secretary of the Bookmakers' Committee with effect from 1st January 1971 on similar lines to those other increases approved by the Board at the July meeting. This was the fourth occasion on which the Chairman discriminated against me on the subject of my pay.

This account is in bare outline only and ignores numerous incidents which only served to undermine my position with the Board. Despite everything I have for most of my service held some responsibility for approximately half the Board's expenditure, and it can be seen from the instruction on Expenditure and Revenue Votes of 9th November 1970 that

I am the only executive with responsibilities in all three distributive fields laid down in the 1963 Act. I am also the only executive who obtained a job with the Board in open competition through a public advertisement and who at the same time can claim a genuine interest in the Board's work.

Appendix II

Retirement Speech to the Horserace Betting Levy Board
The Stafford Hotel, Thursday 25 July 1991

CHAIRMAN, Members of the Board, Ladies and Gentlemen, I am immensely grateful to you all for the Honour you have done me this evening which is an occasion I will always remember with gratitude.

My 28 years with the Board should, however, be placed in perspective when I tell you that earlier this year the Hall Porter of my Club retired and that he started his service in 1921, seven years before I was born. Among his rewards was a lunch in the Members' Dining Room with the Secretary. Such is the way that the British attend to these things.

I joined in March 1963. I had been a substantial punter. I began racing at Newmarket after the war where I was confined to Tattersalls since in those days you could not go into the Members' Enclosure at Newmarket unless you were signed in by a Member of the Jockey Club. Attendances then were very large but I always remember Phil Bull whose beard was flaming red striding from the paddock to the ring. He too was confined to Tattersalls! I had opened a credit account with Ladbrokes who were then doubly represented on the rails. Lower down was the first lady bookmaker who went by the name of Mrs Helen Vernet. She was immensely dignified and sat elegantly on her shooting stick. You were not supposed to have more than £10 with her and even then she would say 'Are you sure you should bet so much?'. Further up the rails was Mr Molony who welcomed more substantial wagers and he was the predecessor of Dickie Gaskell who in turn preceded Peter George. My alert mind enabled me to win more often than I lost, and I soon extended my activities to include Hills, Laurie Wallis, Heathorns and Tote Investors as it then was, and the game used to be to see if I could win off all of them in the same week. The scheme was always to bet in a way which was unattractive to the bookmaker; never on handicaps and usually at odds-on or the favourite for a place at the Tote return. For years I was largely successful but I eventually lost it all when breaking my own rules and doubling up at Cheltenham when not a single favourite obliged. Every bet was recorded and among my treasured possessions was a registered letter from Hills closing my account in which they said, 'the business you bring is of no value to the firm'. Betting on any scale had to end when I married and I foolishly told my wife that Laurie Wallis sent out losing accounts on Tuesday and cheques on Wednesday. She became a dab hand at intercepting the post and identifying winning weeks from losers. I subsequently destroyed all records including the William Hill letter because I became ashamed of my three figure bets and I did not wish the truth to be discovered by my son.

I had, however, bought the knowledge which landed me the most fascinating job anyone could ask for and the bookmakers have been paying me ever since. I think that Michael Wallis and Peter George who had been regular sparring partners were quite pleased to see me working here as there was at least someone who spoke their language.

During my service I have at some time or other been

responsible for every Levy Board activity except for collecting the levy, but my particular joy has been administering the grants for the improvement of the breed and for veterinary science and veterinary education which have been almost my sole responsibility since the day I arrived. I am obviously proud that both have been outstandingly successful and it is rather sad that this success has largely passed you by, but you too should be proud that the Board is held in high regard by everyone connected with these activities. Our assistance in both spheres is absolutely vital, and the smaller the grant the more important it is. The revival in heavy horse breeding stems directly from our support and it was immensely rewarding to see no less than 12 four-horse teams of Clydesdales, Shires and Percherons at the East of England Show a few days ago. This would have been impossible in 1964. In view of the Board's financial situation I have been in touch with all the societies to explain the circumstances so that no applications for increased grants should be received during the next two years, and this will mean that some societies will not have received any review for six years. I do, however, hope that the existing grants can be maintained as they are so vital to the breeders concerned.

Our support in the veterinary field has also been outstandingly successful and has provided for research which has been recognised internationally. Thanks to the Board major advances have been made in the diagnosis of disease and in the treatment of most forms of injury.

Both the work of the Equine Virology Unit at the Animal Health Trust and the Equine Fertility Unit of the TBA are outstanding examples of achievements which have been substantially funded by the Board.

At this point I must pay tribute to the Veterinary Advisory Committee and to the Horserace Scientific Advisory Committee both of which are indispensable and involve a great deal of correspondence. I have enjoyed the happiest relationships with all four Chairmen of the VAC, and with Bob Smith, the Chairman of HSAC, all of whom have given us unstinting service. I must pay particular tribute to Lawson Soulsby and to Bob Smith whose contributions in their respective fields have been outstanding, and how pleased we are that they can be with us tonight.

I must thank many people for their kindness and for their tributes to me now that the time has come for me to depart. I am so pleased to see Andrew Higgins here from the Animal Health Trust and Neville Dunnett from HFL, and also of course Peter Rossdale, a key member of our VAC, whom I invited as a personal guest. I have been given some magnificent presents by those with whom I have worked and I have so appreciated the many letters which I have received from individuals, Associations and Societies. I am grateful to them all.

I would like to thank the Staff and the executives of the Board with whom I have worked so amicably for so long. In particular I would like to thank Ian Beresford who has been my assistant for six years and who has given me such loyal support when I needed it most, and whose knowledge of the scientific world will be invaluable to Libby Archer as she continues to find her way around. Above all I thank Tristram for all his support and encouragement over so many years. He is the outstanding administrator, respected by us all, and I am particularly grateful to him for allowing me the latitude to discharge my responsibilities without interference. I recommend him to give the same support to my very capable successor, Libby Archer, who has learned more in a month than I would have believed possible. Tristram will have his hands full with the problems of 59 racecourses and I do not recommend him to try to absorb 59 research grants as well. I would like to feel that I have been of more value to Tristram when we have disagreed than when we have been at one. There are occasions when you are of no value unless you put your head above the parapet and I hope he has learned something from me in the same way that I have learned much from him.

I am very conscious of the honour which has been bestowed on me by the veterinary profession who have made me an Honorary Member of BEVA, and I am deeply touched by those vets and scientists who are arranging yet another dinner in my honour at the Jockey Club next week. Nobody could have been given a better send off than I have, and I have been truly rewarded for any contribution which I may have made to your affairs.

I could, of course, finish here but there are still a couple of things I must add. I have attended so many meetings in all the forums that I hope you would not wish to prejudice my final comments before I sit down. Racing is part of our heritage and we must not let it down. Racing is bigger than the Jockey Club, the Levy Board, the Bookmakers Committee or any of the Associations and racing means everything from Royal Ascot to Cartmel or Bangor-on-Dee. So many of our apparent difficulties have been around for far too long and some of them could have been disposed of years ago. I have therefore one message for the Jockey Club and one for the Board. To the Jockey Club I say find a place in your Membership for at least one veterinary surgeon on an on-going basis. The contribution to racing from the veterinary profession has never been adequately recognised and you should not have allowed the House of Lords to steal a march on you – for once the Government got something right.

To the Board I suggest that you have really got to fight, and I mean fight, for racing. There have been 12 Home Secretaries since the Board was established and I would not rate their combined interest or contribution very highly. Only one has really gone out of his way to help the Board and that was Roy Jenkins, and if you want to know what he did you will have to buy a copy of my book. The only hint I will give you is that it had nothing to do with levy disputes. The Government is involved with racing whether it likes it or not as it is the largest beneficiary of the system known as MOLMOT. I think that our expertise and our administrative skills should be directed in the one way in which total unanimity is assured and that is by striving for a reduction in general betting duty, with the objective of providing more for racing and alleviating the punter. It is not a forlorn hope. Nobody really anticipated the abolition of on-course betting duty which has done much to stimulate racecourse attendances. This arose more from an initiative by the Chancellor of the Exchequer than from any cohesive submissions from racing. It should be possible to prove that a reduction in GBD will yield an increase in betting turnover which will benefit the Government, bookmakers and racing alike. We are after all the Government's own creation and leadership from this quarter is more likely to receive a hearing than from any other. It may take several years but there are 100,000 people out there, quite apart from racegoers, who will rally to the call and whoever provides the leadership will be indispensable to the entire racing and betting industries.

Chairman, Ladies and gentlemen, I am so grateful to you for making this such a memorable evening in my life. Thank you for listening to me and of course I wish you well.

25 July 1991

Appendix III

Letters in Facsimile

HORSERACE BETTING LEVY BOARD
(BETTING, GAMING AND LOTTERIES ACT 1963)
163, EUSTON ROAD, LONDON, N.W.1.

FIELD-MARSHAL LORD HARDING, CHAIRMAN
SIR RUPERT BRAZIER-CREAGH, SECRETARY

TELEPHONE: EUSTON 2536 (3 LINES)
TELEGRAMS: LEVYBOARD, NORWEST, LONDON

BLB.5062

27 January, 1964.

RACECOURSE CIRCULAR NO. 4(64)

Dear Sir,

    I have to inform you that owing to ill-health Brigadier O.G. Brooke, Assistant Secretary, has unfortunately been forced to tender his resignation from the Staff of the Levy Board.

    In future matters which were previously referred to Brigadier Brooke will be dealt with by Mr. M.R.C. Crawshay Deputy Assistant Secretary.

                                Yours faithfully,

                                      Secretary.

DISTR.
    ALL RACECOURSES.

TEL. GAULDRY 247

1/4/73.

KILMANY,
CUPAR,
FIFE.

Dear Martin

Thank you for your letter of March 29ᵗʰ.

I am so glad you have had an opportunity of a personal talk to our Chairman.

Yrs sincerely

Kilmany

Lets have a word together at the Vet's Conference.

If you want me to talk to the Chairman I will do so when he comes to Kilmany on April 17^{a}.

I remain of the opinion that his talk to you about your affairs should emanate from him — without prompting by me or anybody else, but I agree with you that you cannot wait for ever.

K.

Personal.   11/4/73.

Dear Martin

Well done with the Vets, I thought it went well and, in particular, thank you for looking after me.

We did not, as things turned out, have an opportunity of talking to eachother — nor will we have an opportunity on Monday.

I would still prefer the

initiative to come from the Chairman.

I will, however, do the best I can to put the idea into his head — but all <u>very gently</u>, because I don't know him at all well yet.

Let me repeat that I myself am on your side.

J. M. K.

House of Lords

27/1/75.

Dear Martin

Thank you very much for your letter. I had, in fact, heard your good news when sitting next to the Chairman at dinner last Monday. That it should have taken so long for you to establish your rights made me — as you know — quite indignant quite often, but my

indignation achieved nothing!
Within a month of my departure,
however, 'the penny drops' and all is
well! I am so delighted for your
sake.
All good wishes
Sincerely
Kilmany

Perhaps we may meet at Sandown.

Index

Adderson, Tom and Florrie 2
Allday, Ken 77
Allen, Professor Twink 121, 122
Archer, Libby 119, 153, 154
Astor, Jakie 85
Attlee, Clement 101

Bateman, H.M. 16
Beale, Frank 99
Beresford, Ian 113
Bevan, Tom and Sighle 66
Bey, Giles 39
Bird, Roy 88
Blair, Tony 133
Boyle, Sir Edward 20
Brazier-Creagh, Major-General,
   Sir Rupert 51, 54, 56, 59-64, 71, 90,
   91, 109, 138-141
Brooke, Oliver 53, 57, 60, 61, 138, 139
Bull, Phil 150
Bullivant, Anthony 45
Burrell, Peter 77, 121
Butler, R.A. 55
Buxton, Barbara 66

Campbell, Sir Ronald 39
Carlisle, Mark 79
Carr, Robert 85
Carter, Jack 69
Catchpole, Bernard 62, 64, 72, 73,
   138, 140
Chamberlain, Neville 11, 14
Collins, Christopher 99
Crathorne, Lord 80, 98
Crawshay, Ann 15, 50

Crawshay, Charles I 3
Crawshay, Charles II 109, 137
Crawshay, Elisabeth 53
Crawshay, Emma 43
Crawshay, Grania 66, 76, 119-122,
   129, 130, 136, 137
Crawshay, Huw and Philippa 50
Crawshay, Julian 4, 15, 25, 44, 50
Crawshay, Richard I 1
Crawshay, Richard II 2, 3
Crawshay, Virginia 14, 15
Crawshay, William I 2
Crawshay, William II 2
Crawshay, Sir William 49, 50
Cripps, Sir Stafford 101
Cruso, Francis 17

Davies, John 42
De Walden, Lord Howard 108
Dolan, Pat 61
Dring, William 45
Dunnett, Neville 153

Edinburgh, Prince Philip, Duke of 39
Evans, Professor Sir David 113

Falcon, Michael 11
Falkender, Lady 68
Feilden, Major-General Sir Randle
   69, 80, 90
Fraser, Alistair 114, 116
Freedman, Louis 99

Gaskell, Dickie 151
George, Peter 151

Gisborough, Richard, Lord 24, 46, 50
Gisborough, Shane, Lady 50
Goldsmid, Sir Henry D'Avigdor 79
Goldsmid, John and Ginny 50
Gwynne, Teddy 26

Hadden, Gordon 73
Hambro, J.O. 70
Hancock, Malcolm 78
Hannay, Lennox 16, 26, 50, 137
Harding, Field Marshal, Lord 55-57, 61-67, 69-72, 76, 83, 85, 90, 139, 141, 142
Hartley, Grizel 19
Hartley, Hubert 17, 19
Hay, J.B. 143
Healy, Margaret 104
Heath, Edward 79
Henderson, Sir William 113
Hickman, John 114
Hicks, Sir Denys 81-83, 91, 92, 94, 95, 97, 102, 138
Higgins, Andrew 153
Holland, Peter 36
Holmpatrick, James, Lord 37, 38
Howard, Colonel Cecil 32
Hunt, Michael 114

Jenkins, Roy 85

Kaye, Audrey 42
Kaye, Douglas 41
Keeler, Christine 68
Keown-Boyd, David 38
Kerry, A.H.G. 20
Kilmany, Lord 72, 73, 80, 83, 87-89, 92-95, 98, 103, 104
Kitson, Sir Timothy 79

Mahaffey, Leo 114
Makarios, Archbishop 56
Manton, Lord 80
Margadale, Lord 133
Marriage, John 86
Marshall, RSM W.C. 45

Martin, Hilda 48, 49
Massey, Paul 72, 77, 148
Maudling, Reginald 76
Macdonald-Buchanan, John 106
McKenna, Reg 70, 73, 102
McLeod, David 45
Meades, Margaret 74, 78-80, 94, 95, 102, 108
Molony, Tim 151
Mullion, Mrs Meg 61
Mumford, Dr Jenny 121, 122
Munro, Grant 81

Norfolk, Duke of 56, 75

Osborne, Brian 14
Owen, John 120

Petch, Major Leslie 78
Plowright, Walter 122
Plummer, Sir Desmond, (later Lord) 34, 101-105, 107-109, 110, 119
Pownall, John 45, 46
Prendergast, Paddy 61
Price, Michael 45, 46
Prior, Jim, Lord 12, 13
Profumo, Jack 68

Queen, Her Majesty the 44-46

Raymond, Sir Stanley 84-86, 88, 89, 93, 98, 99, 100
Ricketts, Tristram 101, 102, 104, 107-110, 118, 119, 153, 154
Ritchie, Sir John 58, 80, 93, 96, 99, 104, 113
Robinson, Christopher 46, 123
Robinson, David 75
Rosebery, Lord 56
Rossdale, Peter 114-116, 121, 153
Rothschild, Lord 105, 108
Russell, Tom 72, 73

Sefton, Lord 76
Shinwell, Emanuel 67

INDEX

Silver, Ian 114
Sim, Sir Alexander 70, 91
Singleton, Brian 122
Smith, Professor Bob 153
Somerleyton, Belinda, Lady 123, 125, 127
Somerleyton, Bill, Lord 123
Soulsby, Professor, Lord 113, 153
Sparrow, Sir John 121
Spurgeon, J.F. 10, 11, 13
Stewart, Donald 87, 102

Thomas, Elspeth 129
Tollemache, Michael 123
Trethowan, Sir Ian 109, 110, 113, 114, 119

van den Arend, Sophia 127, 129

Van Royan, Trooper 40
Vernet, Mrs Helen 150
Victory, Paddy 60, 62-64, 72, 74, 77-80, 83, 87, 90, 91

Wade, David 47-49
Wakerell, Leslie 125
Waller, Sam 63-65, 72, 73, 90, 91
Wallis, Michael 151
Ward, Antonia 137
West, David 10
Whitbread, Colonel Bill 88, 89
Wigg, Lord 55, 67-70, 72, 73, 75-81, 83-88, 90, 96
Wilkinson, M.E. 10
Wilson, Harold 68
Wootton, Tony 42
Wyatt, Woodrow 121